WHAT PEOPLE A̶

THE END

The End of Death is a testimonial to the existence of consciousness independent of the brain as well as a wake-up call to the true purpose of life. Admir Serrano tells many compelling stories about those who have had near-death experiences and, as a direct result, transformed their lives. Each one learned this life is a school where we deepen our ability to be compassionate and wise. Serrano encourages us to take in this perspective. His message is a gift of loving-kindness.

Emma Bragdon, PhD, author of *The Call of Spiritual Emergency: From Personal Crisis to Personal Transformation,* and several other books, founder and director of the Spiritual Alliances Foundation

Near-death experience is a scientific fact that has been approached by renowned scientists such as Drs. Raymond Moody Jr., Sam Parnia, and others. However, no one has ever brought the spiritual take from this occurrence in life. Mr. Serrano wisely bridges Science and Spirituality. *The End of Death* goes beyond evidence; it brings comfort and a new perspective of life to the reader.

Vanessa Anseloni, PsyD, PhD, Editor-in-chief of the *Spiritist Magazine*

The End of Death by Admir Serrano brings important information to those seeking answers while exploring their grief. Knowledge, reason and trust are key as we build the group's wisdom, and *The End of Death* offers exactly that, plus the comfort that comes from abolishing the mystery of death.

Luis Salazar, Bereavement Support Group Facilitator

The End of Death

How Near-Death Experiences
Prove the Afterlife

The End of Death

How Near-Death Experiences
Prove the Afterlife

Admir Serrano

BOOKS

Winchester, UK
Washington, USA

First published by Sixth Books, 2013
Sixth Books is an imprint of John Hunt Publishing Ltd., Laurel House, Station Approach,
Alresford, Hants, SO24 9JH, UK
office1@jhpbooks.net
www.johnhuntpublishing.com
www.6th-books.com

For distributor details and how to order please visit the 'Ordering' section on our website.

A CIP catalogue record for this book is available from the British Library.

Design: Lee Nash

Printed and bound by CPI Group (UK) Ltd, Croydon, CR0 4YY

We operate a distinctive and ethical publishing philosophy in all
areas of our business, from our global network of authors to
production and worldwide distribution.

CONTENTS

I dedicate this book to all my evolutionary mates. To every person who has come in and out of my life, for each one gave me the opportunity to learn and to grow. And learning and growing are the reasons we all live for.

Introduction

Perhaps you are reading this book because you have had a near-death experience (NDE) and want to understand what happened to you. Was it true that you left your body for the most incredible trip of your life? On the other hand, you may be mourning a departed loved one and are searching for reassurance that he or she lives on somewhere somehow. Possibly, you have been diagnosed with a terminal illness and could use some comfort knowing that *you* will live on somewhere somehow. Perhaps you already believe that you will go on living after the death of your body but additional evidence could strengthen what you already know. Or you may be skeptical of all this afterlife and immortality *hogwash* and are reading this book because... Because your skepticism is wavering and you—like every other human being on earth—want to know if you will continue living after *you* die. And this is a good thing. If you discover now that you are immortal, your life can change dramatically, for the better. You will know it eventually, but the sooner you do, the quicker you can repair what is wrong and make *this* life a more pleasant experience. Whatever the reason may be, I am glad you are reading it. For this can be the beginning of a long and marvelous journey of self-discovery as you seek your true nature by asking that perennial question, "Who am I—really?" I hope what you read here will convince you at least of one thing—that you are much greater, more valuable, and longer lasting than you may think you are!

As for me, I do not believe we are immortal—I *know* we are. I do not believe we have an extra-physical, I prefer *spirit*, body that can live independently of the physical body—I *know* we do. I do not believe the afterlife is real—I *know* it is real. Therefore, throughout this book I will not hesitate to emphasize repeatedly our immortality and the existence of an afterlife.

If you have read other works on NDE, especially those written by brain scientists, you seldom—if ever—saw the word *spirit* in their writings to refer to that non-physical portion of a human being. *Spirit* is a forbidden word in the erudite circle of materialistic scientists. It is too superstitious a word and its use may cost scientists their tenure. Thus, they run from it, as we would say in my native Brazil, as the devil runs from the cross. Yet *spirit* (from Latin *breath)* is a beautiful word, defined as the vital principle, the essential nature of a person, the animating force within all living things—you, me and erudite scientists included. *Spirit* is also defined as *incorporeal consciousness.* While *incorporeal* is also blasphemy in scientific circles, *consciousness* keeps scientists employed, thus the term they use. If you do not feel too comfortable either with the term *spirit,* you can understand it as *consciousness,* even if your job is not on the line. Throughout this book, I will use *consciousness* mainly to refer to mental or cognitive processes, and *spirit* to refer to the surviving part of our nature, and I might use it interchangeably with *spirit* at times.

The End of Death is my first book in the English language. In it, I share my own experiences on the other side of life, as well as show evidence of an afterlife from people who have had a brush with death and experienced the NDE phenomenon. I have been studying, writing about and lecturing on NDE and life after death for over fifteen years. NDE has been scientifically studied for more than three decades, primarily in the US and Europe. Skeptics and non-believers try to relegate these experiences to some sort of brain anomaly, fantasy, or hallucination. However, regardless how hard they try to dismiss NDE as nothing supernatural, no explanation other than the existence of a spiritual side of us and an afterlife can best account for them.

Though I have had a close call with death myself, I do not recall having a NDE. I was an infant then, back in my home country, when I suffered third degree burns on the upper part of my body. The burns were so severe that doctors told my parents to prepare my funeral. I was dying. As you can tell, they were wrong. Yet I know what NDE is like. NDE is a deeper and more extensive type of out-of-body experience (OBE). While NDE normally happens to a person once, two or three times in extremely few cases, my OBEs happen often. Thus, when I discuss the stages of a full-blown NDE, for instance, I know what a NDE feels like. And I know they are not fantasy, hallucination, or dreams—they are real. And they are real because we are immortal beings, and we have an indestructible body capable of functioning independently of the physical counterpart. So indestructible that it will survive physical death.

Throughout this book, as mentioned earlier, I will refer to this indestructible body as *spirit body*, sometimes as *consciousness*, or *extra-physical* body. Whichever term I use, I will be referring to that part of our nature which survives bodily death, and wherein our identity is indelibly recorded. Our physical body is mortal, as we well know, but that is not who or what we are. Our physical body is a wonderful instrument we use while living on earth, which allows us to experience material life as intensely as we do. It is what gives us the ability to interact with things physical so that we can grow spiritually. The time we spend on earthly life depends on what we have to learn or to teach. It could be just a few hours after we are physically born, or a few days, or over a hundred years. Regardless of how long we stay, we will have to return to the spirit world, which is our true home. NDE is a prelude to what will happen to us when we finish our earthly work. And NDErs (people who go through a NDE) are messengers who experience the reality of the spiritual world and return to tell us about it.

There is a spiritual world, more real than the physical one we know, as NDErs tell us. And I have been there myself. You have been there too already, more times than you can count, but you may not remember it. Our loved ones, who we say are dead, are alive, quite alive in the spiritual side of life, as NDErs tell us. And

I know they tell the truth; I have met my loved ones there several times. And you have met yours as well, but you may not recall it.

Even a skeptic reading the NDE accounts in this book will see that in every human being there is something that transcends physical life and survives bodily death. And here I must make a confession. I was a skeptic once. I used to believe my life was confined within the meager time between my birth and my death, and that *I* was contained inside my physical body. I used to believe that when my body died, *I* would die with it, and would be thrown into an eternal nothingness, ceasing to exist completely. I saw this mistaken belief cast asunder when something extraordinary began to happen to me almost every night. In those experiences, I knew that my body was asleep in my bedroom in Miami. However, some part of me, with all its mental faculties intact, in full awareness of what was happening, and in a body as real as the physical, would escape physical life. In this new body I would find myself in some part of Brazil, or in Egypt—floating in front of the Sphinx in broad daylight (their time, since it was dawn in Miami)—or above Saint Peter's Basilica in Rome, or in many other parts of the earth and in space. I then came to discover that this part of me which travels through the physical and spiritual dimensions as my body sleeps is the true *I*, my real essence. And the second body, which is capable of leaving its physical encasement and venturing through the firmament, is my spirit body, which continues living, thinking, feeling, and acting even without—in fact, better without—the physical body which rests motionless in my bed.

And this is exactly what happens during a NDE. As the physical body is extremely debilitated, clinically dead in a large part of such experiences, the spirit body leaves it momentarily. Carrying with it all the five senses and more, NDErs are able to see with clarity what happens around them while medical personnel work on reviving their physical body. They hear conversations doctors and nurses engage in. And no longer subject to the law of gravity, rise up, floating in the air with the lightness of a helium balloon. Vibrating in higher frequencies than physical matter, walls and ceilings are no obstacles to this new body. Thus, NDErs might leave the physical environment and for a while regain the freedom all of us will experience when death finally frees us from the bonds of matter. As NDErs reach the spiritual dimensions with which they are attuned, they might meet departed loved ones; they might also meet spirit guides, review their lives back on earth and see their mistakes. However, since it is not their time to leave physical life yet, the body is revived and they return to it. They are no longer the same as before the NDE. Something powerful has taken place. There is now an enhanced perception of the meaning of earthly life and their place in it. The glimpse of the spiritual world will stay clearly on their mind, and will be cherished and remembered with charged emotions.

Now I invite you to join me and follow the fascinating flights to the beyond experienced by our NDErs; some radiant, lovely trips; others dark, terrifying experiences. But all filled with lessons we can learn from and use to make our own earthly experience a little better in this magnificent journey called life—which never ends, even if we believe otherwise.

Chapter 1

We Are More Than Human

Celi was my cousin. For over two months, she dangled on the tenuous line separating this life and the next. She had gone to the hospital for a minor surgery, in Jaú, a city in the state of São Paulo, where she lived. Something went wrong and she got such a severe and widespread infection that it destroyed half of her stomach, one lung, the spleen, and a rib, all of which had to be removed as a desperate measure to contain the infection because no antibiotics worked. She spent most of those two months in the intensive-care unit (ICU), comatose. On three occasions, the doctors called family members to come for their final goodbyes— Celi was dying.

I interviewed her two weeks after her "miraculous" cure, in the words of the chief physician. He could not find a medical explanation to account for her survival. He could not find it because he did not see what was happening on the other side of reality as her body lay in the ICU. But Celi could see, so she knew why she survived.

Our first chat was on the phone, since I was in Miami and she was in Brazil. The second was in person when I visited her in Jaú a few months later. Celi was aware of my research on parapsychology and the afterlife so she spoke freely about her experience.

"Some people in a coma," I started, "at times say they were not really unconscious, that they could see and hear things that happened around them. While you were in the ICU, did anything similar happen to you, or were you completely blacked out?"

I heard a labored chuckle on the other end of the line.

"I saw and heard things," she said.

Having followed her condition through one of her brothers, I knew Celi had been heavily sedated while in the ICU.

"But you were unconscious," I said. "How could you have seen or heard anything?"

There was another chuckle. Having had such an experience myself and studied the phenomenon for many years, what she said was no surprise.

"I was outside."

I knew what she meant, but feigned ignorance. "What do you mean outside? You were unconscious in the ICU."

"I was standing by the door."

"But you were in a coma."

"Yeah, but I could see and hear."

"Lying in bed?"

"No, standing by the door."

She spoke slowly. The severe pain plaguing her would get in the way. Several times I asked if she wanted to stop, but she did not, so we continued.

"Were you inside or outside the ICU?"

"Inside."

"What did first draw your attention when you were out?" I asked.

"The body on the bed."

"Did you recognize it as being your body?"

"Yeah."

"Can you tell me about the body?"

"It was intubated and had cables connected to monitors."

By what Celi told me she had spent most if not the entire time out of her physical body while it was comatose. She even said that when medical personnel would come in for their rounds, she would step aside to get out of their way.

"Which of the two did you think you were—the body on the bed or the *you* outside?"

She chuckled again. "It was strange. The one outside, I guess."

Celi's is one of the most fantastic near-death experiences I have come across in the many years I have studied the phenomenon, and we shall revisit it where pertinent as we go on.

More Than the Eyes Can See

We are not the physical body we see in the mirror every day. Neither was Celi the comatose body in that hospital bed; she was the being outside it, spiritual and eternal. And so is each one of us. To the physical body we are just tenants, occupying it until the assigned time of our earthly existence is over. When it is over the body dies and we are out, lively as ever.

The physical body is governed by two energy forces — organic and spiritual; call it consciousness, if you prefer. "Without the slightest doubt there is something through which material (organic) and spiritual energy (force) hold together and are complementary."[1] The organic force maintains the physical organs alive and functioning, while the spiritual force gives it vitality, the power of motion, intelligence, consciousness, character, personality traits, psychic abilities, talents; in a word, all those elements that are part of us which are not physically based. The spiritual force impregnates every atom, cell, molecule and organ of the physical body, organizing it as a coherent unit. In reality, the spiritual force is the matrix molding the physical body, which it permeates, surrounds, energizes, holds together and compels "atoms and molecules to assume — and to retain through constant changes of material — stable arrangements."[2]

Scientists of the sixteenth and seventeenth centuries called the spiritual force within physical organisms vitalism. Vitalists, as they were called, believed that living beings contained a vital force that was independent of the body and infused life into it, a conscious soul or spirit which creates the body and functions through it.[3] Back in those times for a scientist to endow a human being with a 'spirit' or 'soul' animating a physical body was acceptable. Today it is heresy. But that does not mean contemporary reputable scientists do not believe in the existence of such a non-physical organizing force enmeshed with a physical body. Many do, but they cannot call it 'spirit', unless they are contemplating early retirement and academic disgrace. And those who believe—and many have even tested it in their labs—must create scientific-sounding terms, as far away as possible from that heretic name. For instance, Harold Saxton Burr, a professor of anatomy at Yale University School of Medicine from 1916 to 1956, and an expert in bioelectrodynamics, applied techniques and used sophisticated instruments that "revealed that man—and, in fact, all forms—are ordered and controlled by electro-dynamic fields which can be measured and mapped with precision."[4] Burr called them *fields of life* or L-Fields, for short. "The electro-dynamic field of the body serves as a matrix or mould, which preserves the 'shape' or arrangement of any material poured into it, however often the material may be changed."[5] More recently, English biochemist Rupert Sheldrake, a former fellow of the Royal Society of London, proposed that all living organisms, including us, of course, have within them "morphogenetic fields [which] are responsible for the organization and form of material systems."[6] As you can see, Sheldrake's morphogenetic—he also calls them *morphic*—fields echo Burr's L-fields, with a different name. *Prana* (India), *chi* (China), *ka* (Egypt) and just plain *energy fields* are popular terms associated with that invisible and everlasting force which makes us more than mere mortals materialistic science wants us to believe we are. "There is no concept more familiar to us than that of spirit energy, yet there is none more opaque scientifically."[7]

Regardless of the name given to this spiritual force, it has another particular power. It is capable, by some unknown mechanism, to assemble itself into a spirit body which can function independently of the physical and survive bodily death. *Astral*, *etheric* or *energy* body are popular terms associated with this subtle part of our being. Moreover, as it assembles itself and exits the physical body, it transfers to itself our cognitive abilities and sensory capacities, which are enhanced as we are no longer confined to the grossness and limitations of the material body and physical organs.

It was in this subtle or spirit body that Celi, her true self, manifested while the physical body lay comatose. And it is the existence of this spirit body, its ability to leave the physical counterpart, bringing with it one's cognitive abilities and sensory capacities, that allow people in the imminence of death, such as Celi was, to undergo a near-death experience (NDE), such as she did. Not only does it allow NDE, but also out-of-body experiences (OBE) when a person is healthy.

For better appreciation of the NDE phenomenon, it is important to be acquainted with out-of-body experience, OBE for short. This will help you understand how NDE happens. As the term implies, OBE is the experience of leaving one's physical body. It is by the OBE phenomenon that NDErs are able to see what they see and go where they go during their brush with death. Without an OBE there would be no NDE, since the patient's consciousness or spirit, numbed, would stay stuck in the physical body, rather than freeing itself and venturing out. OBE happens to all of us when we sleep, even if we do not recall it in the morning. It happens in every case of NDE, even if the NDEr is not aware of leaving the body. And it will happen to all of us— without exception—when our physical body dies and we—as immortal spirit that we are—leave it for good. Now let us have some fun with an OBE and see how it works.

Sweet Taste of Freedom

Pretend you are a kid again playing with your Barbie or GI Joe doll and you have magical powers. Cradle your little friend in your hands and bring it close to your face. Pucker up your lips and, as if blowing bubbles, blow gently on the doll's forehead. As you blow, you feel a light squiggle on the palms of your hands;

your doll's body temperature begins to rise; the face turns rosy as blood begins to circulate throughout the little body you are holding. Whereas a few minutes before it was just a rigid piece of plastic, now you feel it soft and squishy. Slight throbbing can be seen in the chest area, tiny twitches on the delicate face. Astonished, you follow the slow upward movement as your little friend begins to raise itself on your palm. Standing up, it stares at you with lively twinkling eyes. And rather than crying as a baby coming to this life would, it draws a smile of gratitude at the miracle you have just performed. "Thank you for giving me the gift of life," you hear in a tiny voice.

As you look admiringly at your new creation, your X-ray vision allows you to see beyond the physical body, better yet, inside the physical body. You see mingled with the skin and interspersed in every cell, every molecule and every physical organ of your lively doll tiny dots of sparkling light. You feel like you are looking at a miniature universe shining with billions of radiant little stars. Looking closer you see that these dots are all connected by some kind of invisible force. You notice on top of the head a dot shining brighter than the others. Curiously, you pinch your magical fingers on it; grabbing a hold, you start pulling it upwards. In amazement of what you are witnessing, you cannot stop pulling; you keep pulling and pulling, all the way up.

Now you notice—not on the doll, but on you—your eyes as big as plums and your jaws dropping to the floor at what you are looking at. You cannot help but saying, "Wow, this is freaky!" You would feel and see in the hand you held your once lively friend a cold and motionless doll, not unlike before you blew life into it. On the other what you have just pulled out, floating in the air just before your eyes, a shiny, lively—more lively!—exact and to your great surprise (perhaps greater to your parents) an unbreakable copy of your now motionless tiny friend. You can tug on the arms, legs, and head, squish it, stomp on it, stab it, throw it against the wall and it would remain intact. If you were a *Star Wars* fan, you would be reminded of one of those three-dimensional holographic images of Princess Leia in those futuristic movies.

Pausing for a second to appreciate this magical moment, you marvel at what you have just done—you have produced an OBE to your little friend. Now pretend your floating friend whispers excitedly to you, "Get out of your body too and let's have some fun!"

"How?" you ask.

"Lie down in your bed, close your eyes, relax deeply and this time I'll pull you out."

You do not think twice. You lie down, close your eyes, and relax deeply and in a few moments, *pop!* out *you* are. Meeting your Barbie or GI Joe floating in front of you, you are ready to go to town. In this body, you can fly into space or visit your *bffs* wherever they are. But before taking off to explore the glorious seeing and unseeing worlds our Creator so generously made for his beloved children, you want to get the hang of this new body.

So you go for a stroll around your house first. Forget opening doors to move from one room to the next. Walk straight ahead. Slow vibrating blocks of matter—walls, doors, furniture, appliances, people—are no match to your new highly vibrating spirit body. You are unstoppable now—and remember unbreakable too—so just walk through them. Material objects are now just shadows on the open road before you.

Moving from one room to the next, you feel an incredible lightness of being. You see a law of physics turned on its head—earth's gravitational pull exerts no power over you. You move as though on a magnetic field, your feet not touching the floor under you, your volition guiding your journey. Amazed, a thought comes to your mind, and no sooner you think of it, it happens.

"I wonder if I could float up!"

And up you are, close to the ceiling. Astounded, you look down—and more astonishment. Whatever this new body is, you can see out of it, even if you are not sure how—regular vision like our physical eyes, or by some other means. And not only vision you have, but hearing too.

"What's going on in that room?" you hear your mom calling.

If you have kids, you know that when they are silent for too long, something is cooking. Your mom may have been cooking something too, especially for you. You had already caught a whiff of it. A delicious batch of freshly baked chocolate chip cookies has just been pulled out of the oven.

"Awesome!" you say to yourself. "In this new body I can float up in the air; I can see, hear, smell, and..."

You had not tried it yet—talk.

Floating down you stand close to your mom, so close that you can hear her heart beating.

"Yummy!" you exclaim. "May I have one, Mommy?"

No reply from mother dear. Not even a quiver.

"Mommy?! I'm talking to you!" you repeat.

You feel like you are talking to the cookie tray. Well, you tried to be polite. The cookies are irresistible; the melting chocolate chips are begging to be eaten, so just grab one.

Uh-oh! You are in trouble. You cannot grab anything. You can see the cookies, you can see the tray holding them, they are right in front of you, and they are real. You check your hands to see if there is something wrong with them. You look on the back of them, turn over and check the palms, you count your fingers, five on each hand, all is normal and just as real. But somehow you are not able to interact with people and things as you did when you were in the physical body. A scary thought flashes through your mind.

"Am I dead?"

Startled, you feel a strange power pulling you out of the kitchen; for a second you go blank; and in an instant, you come to again. Your consciousness, which a few seconds ago was in your spirit body, now is back to the physical counterpart, manifesting itself through the brain. You begin to feel the familiar heaviness of the physical body, your mattress under it. You are happy to have returned to the only life you knew, but now you know there is more. You are beginning to awaken.

Along with your breathing, your heartbeat rate had slowed down when *you* left your physical body. Before you open your eyes, you feel your heart racing in your chest. The abruptness of your return caused it to accelerate. As you open your eyes, you see the ceiling above you. You are back to your cozy room. You have not died, but you caught a glimpse of what it will be like when your body dies. You will live on. You will preserve your own identity and all your senses. You will have trouble communicating with your loved ones who stayed behind, and you will have trouble interacting with material things, but you will continue to exist. You will continue being yourself.

On your own, in that blessed instant, without the dictates of any religious dogma, philosophical thought, or scientific paradigm, you discovered the reality of your immortality. You will never be the same again. You have just realized that you are far greater than you ever thought you were. Such an epiphany can give you a completely new perspective of life; an appreciation for it you never imagined would be possible.

Now that you know what an OBE looks like from the outside, I will tell you what it feels like from the inside. Just turn the page and join me in my journey. Physical life has many perks, but none beats...

Chapter 2

The Perks of Being Free

I went to bed about eleven that night. I was tired, and had a feeling I could produce a conscious OBE. I made myself as comfortable as I could, my arms resting on the sides, palms down. Clearing my mind of mundane thoughts, I concentrated on relaxing, mentally suggesting that every part of my body relax. My objective was to induce the vibrational state to facilitate the exit of the spirit body. This internal vibration feels like a generalized tingling throughout the body, as though you are receiving a mild electric shock but devoid of pain. This is as close an explanation as I can give. The vibrational state is commonly a precursor of an OBE, but an OBE can be effected, which is mostly the case, without its presence. The vibrational state is also felt sometimes when we return to the physical body, as the portion of the spiritual force which was out and away re-enters the physical organs.

When the vibration peaks, the spirit body begins to withdraw, normally from the extremities—toes, feet, legs and so on. It rolls up like a snowball, accumulating energy and moving upwards. As vital energy is removed from a certain part of the body, coldness and catalepsy, or muscular rigidity, set in. Breathing and heartbeat rates also begin to diminish. When this process ends, the entire body becomes cataleptic and cold, and all the energy accumulates in the head. There is no pain or discomfort, but you might get scared if you are not familiar with it. You feel a sort of pressure in your head, and may hear a buzzing sound, sometimes voices, laughs, music or your name being called. At the height of the pressure, you sense that something wants to eject through your head. But you remain conscious and capable of thinking, reasoning, making decisions and so on. As long as your consciousness remains physically focused, you are aware of your body even though it is cold and cataleptic; you can also sense your physical environment—your bed, your room etc. The longest part of inducing a conscious OBE is establishing the vibrational state, which can take a few minutes or a few hours, if you have the patience, but the rest is fast, a matter of minutes or seconds even.

It took me about fifteen minutes to achieve the vibrational state and to be ready to leave. When you know that you are about to leave your body, if you fix your thought on a place or a person you want to visit, most likely you'll land there. You may have heard of people saying a loved one appeared to them in spirit, and later discovered that person had just died. If someone you care about appears to you at the moment of her or his death, be thankful; you were uppermost on that person's mind right before her or his earthly departure.

In my case, I fixed my mind on visiting my sister in São Paulo, Brazil, over 4,000 miles from Miami. I heard the familiar pop as I exited through the forehead, and was at her house— instantly. I landed outside the front door, down a flight of stairs on the side entrance. I am familiar with the house; I had lived there before coming to the US. It had been about nine years since I last saw my sister. I knew, of course, that the closed door was no obstacle, so I went through it unhesitantly. There are two bedrooms in the house, but somehow I went straight to the one she was in. My sister is single and was sleeping alone, but I saw two bodies in her bed, which was no surprise. Her physical body grounded to the bed, and the spirit counterpart suspended a few inches above it. If her physical body had been uncovered, I would have been looking at a crooked X, the physical laying vertically beneath the slightly transversal spirit body. One side of the X was physical head and spirit feet, and the other physical feet and spirit head.

Something else drew my attention, both heads, physical and

spiritual, were wrapped in a sort of white bandage. I was looking at this scene standing by the door, and in a sort of a diving motion, I floated over to her. Embracing her spirit body, I told her I missed her and loved her. Being awake in her spirit body, we carried on a brief conversation. I was completely *lucid*, aware that I was out of my body, thus knew I had a physical body lying inert in Miami, but the real me was in Brazil, rejoicing in my sister's company.

In a state of heightened lucidity when our physical body dies, we know we no longer belong to the earth side of life. Knowing this we can then embark on the next great adventure awaiting every soul who finishes its earthly journey. Otherwise, we may stay earthbound or even stuck to the decomposing physical body, unaware of what has happened to us until the light of that new reality shines on our dormant consciousness.

Thus knowing that I was out of my body, insistently I told my sister that she was not dreaming, that I was indeed there paying her a visit. I also told her that I would call in the morning and would ask if she remembered my visit. Though curious about the bandage on her heads, for some reason I did not ask her about it then. This OBE happened about eleven-twenty at night our Miami time, two-thirty in the morning in São Paulo; due to the time difference it was three hours ahead of us. I called my sister in the morning but she did not remember anything. And I forgot to mention the bandage on her head.

We had lived together for many years during our childhood and part of our adult life, but I had never seen her head wrapped in a bandage before. She has suffered from migraine headaches since she was nine years old, and it kept getting worse as time went on. A couple of years after this OBE I went to Brazil for a tour to promote my first book in Portuguese, and my sister put me up. Normally she was sleeping when I came home at night, so I would see her in the morning. The second or third morning, as I walked past her bedroom, the door was ajar; and she was lying in bed awake. I went in and to my great surprise, her head was wrapped with a white bandage, exactly the way I had seen it during my OBE visit. I asked her about it and she told me that when her migraine is too severe, wrapping the bandage tightly alleviates the pain. I asked her how often she did that, and she said quite often, as it helped her get some sleep. I then told her I had seen it during that night I visited her out of my body.

The fact that even the spirit head showed a bandage wrapped around it should come as no surprise. Either consciously or unconsciously, we do project to the spirit body those elements we hold most strongly on our minds. It could be a simple bandage, like in my sister's case, or even a missing limb in the case of a physically impaired person. Our thoughts and emotions form our reality, both in the physical and spiritual life.

As you noticed in this experience, my body was sleeping in Miami, and I—my true self—out of the physical body, went to my sister's house in Brazil in a split second. She was also out of her body, but had gone nowhere; she was just hanging out in her bedroom—literally. This is a very common occurrence. Even with training, you might get out of your body and not be conscious of it—and you might scare people too. When my older daughter was about nine years old, several mornings she complained to me that I had scared her during the night as she awoke and saw me hovering by the door in her room. She would even describe the clothes I was wearing, more often a particular shirt I liked.

Know Thyself

When I speak about our ability to live independently of the physical body and the existence of a spirit body that survives bodily death, I speak with the certainty of one who has experienced it to some extent. For instance, I have consciously left my body and spent time, on more than one occasion, examining my own spirit body. I looked at my spirit hands, my feet, whether I was wearing clothes—in many cases I was naked even though the physical body was clothed. I have checked if I had my glasses on, and even jumped on my left leg to check if I felt knee pain. I have a deteriorated left knee as a result of a serious injury. Physically it hurts daily, and there is severe pain if I jump on my left leg, but there was no pain on the spirit counterpart.

The Line of Life

As you had 'pulled out' the entire spirit body from your living Barbie or GI Joe doll, holding one in each hand, something would have drawn your attention. You would see a thin silverish line connecting the two bodies, resembling the silk strand of a spider web. Glancing at the extension of the line, you would see one end connected to the nape of your doll's spirit body and the other on the forehead of the physical. And this connecting line was telling you that though the physical body of your doll was motionless and appeared dead, it was still alive. But it was cataleptic, kept alive by the organic force responsible for physical life. The silver line or silver cord, as it is referred to, is the lifeline between the two bodies. And while it is connected, the physical body is alive.

As you learn to identify an OBE during sleep and gain lucidity, you can even, as I often do, reach out to the nape of your spirit head and pull this silver cord, exam it, and ascertain its reality. You can also look back and follow its path as it disappears in the universe, the other end connected to the physical body lying motionless somewhere. I have had OBEs so clear, so profound and so lucid that I was certain my body had died. On one occasion, I was so sure of it that my next thought was trying to figure out how it had died. I have always been in very good health, so the best candidate was a heart attack. But then I reached to the back of my head and the cord was still there. It had not snapped. So I am still here, until the day it snaps.

We do work in the spirit world during our OBE adventures, both in the company of other OBErs and discarnate spirits. On such occasions, I have the habit of reaching out to the nape of my OBE companions to see who is still in physical life. I do this as surreptitiously as I can. One night a companion with no cord noticed and looked at me with a smirk on his face. "Yes, Admir, I'm out of my body," he said, "permanently."

There will be a day when our mortal body will cease its earthly work, and it will die. *It* will die, not us! We are not our physical body. We are immortal beings using the physical body to experience physical life as a means to accelerate our spiritual, moral and intellectual progress. When we pass to our loved ones the burden of burying or cremating our dead body, that is what they will bury or cremate, our dead body—not *us*. We will be alive and free. And may even stick around our own funeral, many a time not understanding what is happening and wondering why people are so sad. Abundant are the cases of family members, especially mothers, who feel the presence of their deceased children in their own funeral, or in their homes later on.

I was a teenager when my father died. As I lay in bed the night after his burial, he hovered over for a final goodbye—scaring the wits out of me. The rest of the night and the following two I slept with my mother.

I did not know then what I know now. All that physical death does to us is free us from the bonds of matter, and the day the body dies, *we* will be risen. That day *we* will return to the spiritual realm from where we all hail. And while our loved ones on this side of life weep in sorrow at our loss, believing we are extinguished forever, our loved ones on the other side—our side now—celebrate in joy our return to the motherland. Rejoicing in this unexpected divine grace, together we will sing the beautiful words Paul the Apostle sent as encouragement to the Corinthian church, for now we understand what they mean. We have just become witnesses of our own immortality.

Behold, I show you a mystery; we shall not all sleep, but we shall all be changed. In a moment, in the twinkling of an eye, at the last trump: for the trumpet shall sound, and the dead shall be raised incorruptible, and we shall be changed. For this corruptible must put on incorruption, and this mortal must put on immortality. So when this corruptible shall have put on incorruption, and this mortal shall have put on immortality, then shall be brought to pass the saying that is written. Death is swallowed up in victory. O death, where is thy sting? O grave, where is thy victory?[1]

If you believe in the authority of the Holy Bible, then you have in the above passage ample reason to know that you are much more than a mere mortal. You can rest assured that when your body takes its last breath after a long and hard earthly mission, you — the real you — will rise out of it, with all your faculties and senses intact. For, in the words of Paul, "There is a natural body, and there is a spiritual body. It is sown a natural body; it is raised a spiritual body."[2]

But in case you want extra reassurance even though you believe in the authority of the Holy Bible, science has already proven the existence of this spiritual body and its ability to leave the physical counterpart. As you will shortly see, the first phase of a full-blown NDE is the feeling of leaving the body, or an OBE, without which, as I said before, there would be no NDE. I have also said that OBE is a very common phenomenon that happens to healthy people all over the world, including you and me.

How can you know if you have had an OBE? There are some signs. For instance, dreams with extreme clarity, especially those where you find yourself happily hanging out with a deceased loved one is a good example; those dreams you say "it was too real to be a dream," are great candidates for OBE. A feeling you cannot move your body, called catalepsy or sleep paralysis, is another; in catalepsy, you, in your spirit body, are very close to the physical counterpart, close enough to feel its rigidity and coldness, but are not entirely *coincided* with it, thus the paralysis.

Falling is another sign that you have been out of your body. If you are falling, you are returning to it following a brief escape from matter after having had a glimpse of your own immortality.

Flying dreams are the most eloquent signs. If you are flying you are out. Flying dreams do not happen inside your head; it is you in your spirit body flying outside, either on the earth plane or the spiritual dimension. In my flying dreams, many of which I produce consciously upon noticing that I am out of my body, I have seen the outside of my house as I returned to my body and the parking lot as I left it. During a hurricane in Miami a few years ago, I found myself flying outside in the middle of the night having a bird's view of the damages. These are just a couple of examples of the many flying dreams I have had which prove to me beyond the shadow of a doubt that flying dreams are not neuronal productions. When we dream that we are flying we are actually out of our body experiencing for a moment our physical independence.

Now let us see what science has to say about OBEs.

Chapter 3

The Science of OBE

I was master of my body. More, I could now also direct the mind to leave my body entirely and roam at will, for after having once established the line of least resistance, the way became easier and the extent of my experiments ever greater. And from the brutal jacket and the dungeon Hell I learned to project myself into the living, breathing outside, the world of today, witnessing events and telling the 'Tiger' about them.

I was present during a shipwreck, just outside the Golden Gate, heard the cries of women and children, saw them swallowed by the sea; and while I stood upon the deck of the ship, one man adjusted a strange apparatus and floated safely away as the vessel sank beneath him. In later years I had that device patented as the 'Morrell Life-Saving Suit'.[1]

This wreck was an actual occurrence as I afterwards found out. It happened on the very day that I had left my body encased in the straightjacket in San Quentin's (prison) dungeon.

At other times, unbelievable as it might seem, my mind was projected outside of the dungeon, playing a part in the lives of people I was later destined to meet, some of whom were to aid materially in my rehabilitation and freedom.

I had become a master of self-hypnosis, suspended animation, call it what you will, and I believe I am one of the few mortals who ever expressed the claim that intelligence endured, or that there was continuity of thought or knowledge of time and events while in this state (out of the body).

During my many sieges of torture in the jacket, nothing occurred in my dungeon cell of which I wasn't aware, though absolutely dead to physical feeling or pain, proving conclusively that my mind was ever in control.

I was indeed the 'Star Rover' of the ages, and Jack London's book just mildly touches upon that prison life of mine, leaving most amazing phenomenon unwritten, the most wonderful of my travels and doings untouched. He called those experiences "the little death." I prefer to call them "my life in tune with a power divine."[2]

This account is just a part of the extraordinary out-of-body experiences of Ed Morrell, a friend of Jack London's. It was Morrell's OBEs during his punishments in a straightjacket in the dungeon of Saint Quentin Prison, for several years in the late 1800s, which inspired London to write *Star Rover*. Morrell says that in several of his out-of-body adventures he would find himself in a classroom in a town of fruit and flowers, standing in front of a girl who sat near the open window.[3] Meeting her by chance upon his release, when the girl was eighteen, they later married. On her side of the story, she said on several occasions she had seen a man wearing a striped prison uniform standing in front of her in class, who would then disappear.

OBE in the Lab

Out-of-body experience is not a recent phenomenon. It is as old as humanity, since we, as spirit, can and do leave the physical body every chance we get. "OBEs have been reported throughout history by individuals from all walks of life...They were known to the (ancient) Egyptians, the North American Indians, the Chinese, the Greek philosophers, the medieval alchemists, the Oceanic peoples, the Hindus, the Hebrews, and the Moslems."[4]

As a science, we can trace experimental OBE investigation back to France in the second half of the nineteenth century. At that time the phenomenon was called somnambulism, not to be confused with sleepwalking. Albert de Rochas, a historian, military engineer, writer and parapsychologist, and Allan Kardec, an educator, writer, and founder of *Spiritism*, were active investigators of both somnambulism and mediumship. However, it was in America in the beginning of the 1960s that OBE experiments were conducted in the lab.

"The first attempts to study OBE scientifically in more contemporary times came only in 1965 when Dr. Charles Tart, a psychologist at the University of California at Davis, turned his attention to the subject."[5] And such attempts were extremely successful as Dr. Tart's subject, Miss Z, a conscious OBEr, correctly identified a five-digit number written on a piece of paper placed on a ledge in the lab. The number written on the paper which she correctly gave was 25132. "The odds against getting a 5-figure random number correct by a single guess are 100,000 to one against. Such long odds suggest very strongly that the number was not guessed, but read paranormally."[6] For these experiments, Miss Z would sleep in a cot in Dr. Tart's sleep lab at the University, hooked up to electrodes monitoring her brain waves and other physiological responses. She would be instructed to sleep and if she got out of her body, she was to float up to the place where the paper was, to read and to memorize the number and then to communicate the answer to the researcher. The correct answer came one morning shortly after six o'clock. Reporting that she just had been out of her body, she correctly recited the entire number to the experimenter. "Even more suggestive was what her brain waves were showing at the critical time. The EEG readings demonstrated that just before calling out over the intercom (to report her OBE), Miss Z slipped from normal sleep into a rather strange and unclassifiable 'drowsy' state that did not represent a clear-cut sleep or waking state. This suggested to Dr. Tart that something more than ESP had been involved in his subject's success."[7] In fact, Dr. Tart's five decades dedicated to consciousness research led him to conclude that:

Thousands, if not millions, of people alive today have had the experience of existing outside the space of their physical bodies for a brief period and experiencing this separated state as *real*, not as a dream or imaginary experience. A typical consequence of such an out-of-body experience is on the order of 'I no longer *believe* that I have a soul, or that some part of me will survive death, I *know* it!'[8]

Though I have had several contacts with Dr. Tart, I have not had the chance to ask him if he has had such experiences himself. But whether he has or not he is absolutely right in his conclusion. This is exactly what the feeling is like. You *know* that you are immortal, and no scientific postulates to the contrary will convince you that you are wrong! You have been there; the naysayers have not (but will be). It is an awesome feeling!

In the early 1970s the Psychical Research Foundation (today Rhine Research Center), associated with Duke University in Durham, North Carolina, conducted a series of OBE experiments more intensely with an OBEr named Keith Harary. Harary had just enrolled as an undergraduate psychology student at Duke and heard that the PFR was looking for volunteers for OBE experiments. He was one of those people who could leave his body at will, so he volunteered. In a series of meticulously controlled and documented experiments, where Harary would be sequestered to a room in the lab and hooked up to EEG and EKG machines, the results of his OBE experiments were astounding.

Have you ever heard that some animals can see ghosts? Well, test results showed that indeed some could. Harary participated in experiments involving different animals, including a kitten and a serpent. For the kitten test Dr. Robert Morris, the experimenter, placed the kitten on a board called an 'animal activity board', a checkered board by which the kitten's activity rate could be monitored, such as the number of squares it would pass in a certain time. The kitten's meowing rate was also carefully observed and recorded. For this experiment, the kitten was placed in the lab and Harary was taken to a room at Duke University Hospital, half a mile away. "This experiment was run several times and the results were simply amazing. The kitten would invariably become very agitated when placed on the board. It would jump about and meow continually. Yet every time [Harary] projected to it, the kitten would suddenly calm down, sit motionless, and would not meow at all. Its change in behavior was often so striking that the investigator monitoring the kitten had little trouble working out just when [Harary] was making his visitations."[9] With the snake it was the opposite. "Before the test and during the experimental period, it was as calm as could be and simply meandered about its cage rather undramatically. The snake seemed to become more agitated at the beginning of the second experimental period. To my amazement, it slid up the side of the cage and literally seemed to attack the side of the terrarium. It bit at it wildly and then—just as mysteriously—calmed back down again."[10] When the experimenters met with Harary afterwards, he said that he had "simply left his body and found himself with us, tried to attract our attention, and then projected right into the terrarium with the snake. The timings between when [Harary] would have been with the reptile, and its radical response, were almost exact."[11]

In another experiment Harary was to leave his body and go to the meditation room in another location. In the meditation room some randomly chosen staff members had been instructed to sit for the experiment. Harary's task was to project to the room and see who was sitting where and give their names, and he did so at first trial—exactly! Not only that. On occasion, some of the members in the meditation room had seen his apparition, even though they did not know when Harary would project there. Keith Harary earned a PhD in psychology from Duke, and is an active investigator of dreams, lucid dreams, and OBE to this day.

The American Society for Psychical Research, founded in 1884 in Boston, Massachusetts, considered the oldest psychical research organization in the US, has been involved in the research of paranormal phenomena, including out-of-body experiences. One such experiment was carried out with Ingo Swann in 1972. Swann was one of the most famous psychics of the 1970s, and could project his consciousness to a hidden target and describe it accurately, wherever it was.[12] Both Swann and Harary worked for the CIA as 'psychic spies' during the project code-named Stargate—and got paid for their services. Sponsored by the US government, the project ran from 1972 through 1995, and was conducted at Stanford Research Institute, Menlo Park, California. Swann, Harary, and a number of psychics who worked in the project during the twenty-three years of its existence were extremely successful in furnishing military and civilian intelligence information they obtained remotely, [13] while out of their bodies.

OBE research is still active today. Currently the largest organization involved in investigation and training is the International Academy of Consciousness (IAC), of which I am a member and where I trained OBE techniques. IAC is an offshoot of the International Institute of Projectiology and Conscientiology (IIPC) founded in 1988 in Brazil by psychic medium, OBEr and OBE investigator Dr. Waldo Vieira. IAC has training and research centers in a number of cities in some seventeen countries, and is open to anyone interested in the subject.

The above are just a few examples of controlled and verified cases of OBE. However, there is much more out there confirming Apostle Paul's assertion that there is a natural body, and there is a spirit body. And this spirit body rises out when the physical body dies and continues its evolution on other realms of reality. When the spirit body rises out from the physical, as you will see in the NDE cases I will be presenting, it brings with it the entire identity of the person; nothing, except organic life, is left in the physical counterpart. And this is because somewhere in the spirit body there is a mental unit where all the memories, experiences, and identity of that person are indelibly recorded. When we are in the physical body during our earthly existence, we manifest ourselves through it, but we can and will function independently of the physical body when we are out. OBEs and NDEs are eloquent examples of this independence.

I hope this has helped familiarize you with a portion of your nature you might never thought existed or paid attention to. That we have a spirit body enmeshed with our physical body. And this spirit body is able to leave the physical counterpart and to act independently of it; and that we will not lose our identity when we are out, be it during an OBE, NDE, or death. That there is a lifeline (silver cord) connecting the two bodies when the physical body is alive. Knowing all this we can better appreciate the profound life-changing phenomenon of near-death experience. We can also learn lessons we can apply to better our own life and make it an easier and more pleasant experience. However, before riding with NDErs to the deeper realms of the spirit world, where our true home is, let us see what NDE really is and who has such transforming experiences.

Let us continue our journey...

Chapter 4

What is Near-Death Experience (NDE)— Really?

Near-death experience (NDE) is a deeper form of OBE that affords the spirit body easier exit from the physical counterpart. And once free from the weight and restrictions imposed by physical organs, the spirit body enjoys greater freedom of movement and enhanced mental capacity. We have seen that the spirit force is enmeshed with the physical body, connected to each atom, each cell, each molecule and each organ that make up the physical body. When the body is healthy and active, the spirit force is tightly connected to the physical organs. And when the body rests, or becomes ill, the connection loosens up, thus facilitating the withdrawal of the spirit body, either partially or completely.

To produce an OBE when the body is healthy, with some exceptions, we need to lie down or sit comfortably to relax the body so that the physical ties can loosen up. During sleep, especially at certain stages of the sleep cycle when the organs are deeply relaxed, it becomes easier. During a brush with death, as in the case of NDE, when the functions that keep the body alive cease temporarily—breathing, heartbeat, blood circulation, brain activity—the disconnection and exit of the spirit body becomes even easier. Easier than during a NDE is when the body dies for good and all physical connections are severed, including the rupture of the silver cord.

The term *near-death experience* was coined by Dr. Raymond Moody in 1975; in his little bestseller book *Life After Life*. Moody called *near-death experience* the unique and spiritually powerful phenomenon many people in the imminence of death may experience. In many cases patients had been declared dead by the attending physicians—the patients' bodies, that is, had been declared dead, not the patients! In fact, many of them out of their body and looking down at the scene from a vantage point, completely conscious though unseen by and unable to attract the attention of the (physically) living, vehemently protested the medical verdict, as you will see shortly.

NDE is often experienced when the patient is clinically dead, though not necessarily. Clinical death occurs when the heart stops beating, in conditions such as cardiac arrest or any other circumstance causing the heart to cease its normal functioning. As the heart stops beating, blood circulation and breathing are interrupted. As you may recall from your human biology class, pumped by the heart, blood circulation is what keeps our physical body alive. Oxygen and vital nutrients are delivered by the blood to our organs and tissues. Blood also removes waste and carbon dioxide from cell metabolism to keep us clean and healthy. To keep our body alive circulation must be a constant, nonstop process, otherwise "… if blood flow were to suddenly stop, you would experience no more than a few seconds of consciousness before blacking out—and then you would have but a few minutes to live."[1]

The reason we would have a few minutes to live if blood flow were to stop would be because the brain would not receive the necessary amount of oxygen to function properly. "The brain… is the body's single largest consumer of oxygen. Although the brain represents only about 2% of the body's weight, it utilizes about 20% of the body's oxygen. As a result, the brain is especially sensitive to hypoxia (suffocation). After about 4 to 6 minutes without oxygen, large numbers of brain cells begin to die. Prolonged hypoxia results in death.[2]

In clinical death, where breathing and heart function are absent, the person becomes, from a physical perspective, if not legally dead yet, at least completely unconscious. Un-consciousness caused by shortage of oxygen to the brain and the consequent cessation of brain activity. If the person were connected to an electrocardiogram (EKG) and/or an electroencephalogram (EEG), these machines, rather than showing the peaks and valleys of normal heartbeats or brain waves, would display a flat line. And a flat line is a sign that the vital activities of the heart and/or the brain came to a halt. In this condition, if timely resuscitation attempts are not successful, unless a miracle of the highest order occurs, which sometimes happens, the person would die.

Until shortly before the first half of the twentieth century, to victims of cardiac arrest death was mostly certain. After this period, cardiopulmonary resuscitation (CPR), adrenaline injection straight into the heart, and other emergency procedures were developed. These new techniques and procedures are capable of re-establishing and normalizing heartbeat, blood flow, and consequently cerebral activity, enabling many patients to resume their earthly life.[3]

To the extent of what medical science knows about human beings, a person whose brain shows no activity cannot feel any sensation, is incapable of motion, is unable to hear and obviously unable to think, to rationalize or to discern anything. No one in this condition could have, according to conventional scientific paradigm, any sign of consciousness. But contrary to what this paradigm postulates, this is not what has happened to millions of people worldwide who have had a brush with death. And this is an eloquent sign that conventional scientific assumptions as relate to our true human— better yet, our spiritual—nature must be carefully revised.

As you already 'experienced' during your make-believe OBE in Chapter 1, and will see shortly in the amazing cases I will be presenting, our consciousness, our identity, the *I* which we truly are, is not enclosed in the brain like a bird in a cage, and when the cage is destroyed the bird dies. The extreme opposite is true! When the cage is destroyed, the bird is free. *We*, the spiritual force we truly are, can and will function independently of the brain and the body and will—*we* will!—survive bodily death.

Having had a glimpse of the afterlife and ascertained their immortality, an immense number of people 'returned' to earthly life after a narrow escape from physical death. And to enlighten us about the world beyond, they were kind and brave enough to share the extraordinary experiences they had while free from the bonds of matter. Their heart had stopped beating; their breathing had ceased; they had lost all brain activities; many flatlined; many declared dead. Therefore, in such a condition, according to medical science, these people could not have seen anything, heard anything, felt anything, or moved anywhere and yet, defying the materialistic view of our human nature, they did it all!

Chapter 5

NDE Everywhere

"In 1975, the world woke up to near-death experiences," wrote Raymond Moody. "They had, most likely, taken place since the beginning of man."[1] Indeed, near-death experience is not a new phenomenon. We, in our spirit body, have left our physical body since we began incarnating. And we do leave it every night as we sleep, whether we are aware of it or not. My sister, for example, had no clue she had been out of her body, perhaps most of the night. Those nights I scared my daughter as she awoke and saw me hanging out in her room, I had no clue I was out of my body either.

Episodes that render the physical body weaker than normal, cardiac arrest, accidents, drowning, and overdose, for example, facilitate the exit of the spirit body and amplify cognitive functions. Therefore, NDErs experience time out of the body with greater clarity and enhanced capacity to retain the memory of what they hear, see, and feel—in both dimensions, the physical as they exit the body and hang around it, and the non-physical, as they venture away from the environment where they are having the life-threatening episode.

What we can consider new about NDE is its increasing publicity as NDErs come out and tell their amazing stories, and the media readily publicize and sensationalize them. And even publication is not that new either. Religious scholar Carol Zaleski, in her book *Otherworld Journeys*, found numerous accounts in medieval literature. But these findings by no means signify that people began to have NDE at that time, of course. What we see there is the historical beginning of case recording.

But why are there so many cases in the present time? The answer is simple. The advances in medicine and resuscitation techniques are enabling more people in the imminence of death to return to physical life. Having had a glimpse of what lies ahead in the life beyond, NDErs are sharing what they have seen. In fact, all of us will have this glimpse eventually, but not all will return to tell. And those returning to tell are people of all ages — children, teenagers, adults, and senior citizens, both male and female, regardless of their social status, intellectual level, be they religious, agnostics or atheists, of all races in every part of the world, whether they believe in life after death or not.

In 1982, when NDE investigation in the US was in its climax, George Gallup, Jr. published the results of polls taken to find out how many Americans had had a NDE episode. In the adult US population alone eight million people who had a brush with death reported some kind of mystical experience associated with the near-death episode.[2] Fifteen years later, in 1997, in a new poll by *US News & World Report* that number had jumped to 15 million — one third of the 45 million who had been in the imminence of death had a NDE episode.[3] Data from the *Near-Death Experience Research Foundation* indicate that in the US alone, there are about 774 cases of NDE — daily![4] According to PMH Atwater, one of the pioneers of NDE research, and a NDEr herself, one in three adults who have had a brush with death had a NDE. Among children, the proportion increases drastically — three in four![5] But why such a huge difference between children and adults? Why would more children than adults have such an experience? Before offering a possibility, I ask your permission to allow me to digress a bit in order to make a point.

Talking to the Dead

You may remember in one of your Sunday School classes the story of King Saul in the first *Book of Samuel*. The day Saul discovered that, outnumbered by the Philistines, his army would be crushed in the looming battle. Afraid and desperate for guidance, "he inquired of the Lord, but the Lord answered him not, neither by dreams, nor by U'rim (divination), nor by prophets."[6] Forsaken by God, the closest to divine help he could get was from a special person—Samuel, his beloved prophet. However, there was a problem; Samuel was dead. Well, not really a problem, just a small inconvenience Saul knew how to circumvent. "Seek me a woman that hath a familiar spirit," he ordered his servant, "that I may go to her and inquire of her."[7] The woman with a familiar spirit was a psychic medium who, endowed with psychic vision and hearing, could see and talk to the (physically) dead and relay their message to the (physically) living. As you recall from that lesson, Saul did talk to Samuel, but what he heard was far from what he was expecting or wanted to hear… "tomorrow shalt thou and thy sons be with me…"[8] And indeed they were. Saul's three sons were killed in battle; he was seriously wounded, and not wanting to die by the hands of the Philistines, "took a sword and fell upon it."[9]

Spirit communication, such as the above example, is as old as humanity as well. As spirit we all are, even when we are incarnated in a physical body, we still have a foot on the other side. You have been in contact with 'dead' people more times than you care to count. However, since it is mostly at night as your body sleeps, you call it a dream. But some incarnated people have—and you may be one of them—greater abilities to communicate with discarnate spirits at will. You may have heard of Arthur Ford, Jane Roberts, John Edward, and James Van Praagh among other famous American mediums.

In Brazil, *Spiritism* is a popular and growing religion, and, brought by Brazilian immigrants it is growing in the US and other parts of world as well. The greatest medium in the Spiritist movement was the late Francisco Xavier. With only a grade-school education, Xavier channeled 412 books in a wide range of subjects, history, religion, philosophy, science, life on earth, life in the beyond are a few of the topics. I am telling you this because I shall be referring to some teachings Xavier received from his spirit guides relevant to some elements in this book, starting where I digressed. Why do more children than adults have NDEs?

Emmanuel, Xavier's spirit guide, tells us the following about children: "Up to seven years of age, the (incarnated) spirit is still in the adaptation phase to the new existence he came to earth to experience. Up to this age the integration (of the spirit element) and organic matter (the material body) is not yet perfected."[10] Now let us put it together during a child's brush with death and see what happens. The spirit element is not in complete connection with the physical body in a child, according to Emmanuel, and that body has lost its vital functions due to a life-threatening condition, or clinical death even. In such a feeble physical condition for a not yet fully integrated spirit to exit the body, it becomes as easy as the detachment of a dandelion seed when blown in the wind. Therefore, from a spiritual perspective, we have here a clear explanation why children report more NDEs than adults do.

Of course, there is no way we can prove whether what Emmanuel is saying is correct. However, there is a commonly occurring phenomenon, in every part of the world where a human being is dying, that adds strength to his statement. Nearly every person in the final stages of a terminal illness who is conscious, or a person of old age whose body is preparing to die, has, what is called in the literature of death and dying, a *deathbed vision* or the more modern term *pre-death experience*. You might have seen a family member or a friend in this stage talking lively and excitedly to a deceased relative or friend present in the room, but whom you could not see. Or, just prior to taking the last breath seeing a beautiful garden, or a radiant green meadow, or of people dressed in white waiting for them on the other side. If you have not, talk to a hospice or nursing home nurse and they will tell you how common this is.

However, if they are still in the physical body, why can they see spirit beings and spiritual places and you, in the room with them, cannot? Because here the opposite of what Emmanuel says about children is taking place. Whereas in a child the spirit element or consciousness is not yet fully integrated, thus facilitating otherworldly perceptions, in the dying stage the same element is in the process of detachment, as the body weakens and prepares to shut down for good. So here, in a way, the spiritual connection is not fully integrated either. In this condition the dying person is straddling realities, pretty much like a child—one foot here and another there—and this gives acuity to their psychic vision, allowing them to glimpse the other side of life even while still here.

The psychic abilities many healthy children display sometimes may originate from this partial liberation of the spirit body. They may be able to foresee future events, to remember past lives, or to interact with discarnate spirits, such as in the case below.

Playmates from the Beyond?

You may have had an imaginary friend or friends as playmates in your lonely childhood days. While it is true that many imaginary friends are just that—imaginary—many are not. I know of a child whose imaginary friend was named *Paulinho*—Little Paul, in Portuguese. This child would have a blast every time Paulinho came around to play with him. His mother would watch in amazement at the good time her son would have—talking, laughing, and playing games— with his imaginary friend.

"Whom are you playing with?" the mother asked one day.

"Paulinho!" he answered. "Do you know Paulinho?" The child thought the mother could see him too.

"No," she replied, "I don't know Paulinho."

One day the mother was showing her son a family photo album. She came to a picture of a man the boy had never seen, "This was your grandfather. He died before you were born."

The boy jumped out of his chair. "This is Paulinho! And you told me you didn't know him!"

The grandfather's name was Paulo, *Paulinho*, the diminutive form, used by the boy as a term of endearment, quite common in Brazil to address close friends or relatives.

If we listen rather than readily dismiss as fantasy what children say that appears imaginary to us, we might learn some interesting things. When my younger daughter was about three years old, we would be playing together in our apartment and all of a sudden she'd stop. Like a little gazelle sniffing danger, she would crane her neck and perk up her ears, little brown eyes wide open but not seeing anything in the room. It was as though a psychic part of her, a second sight, had projected outside.

"Mommy is coming," she would say.

A few moments later, I would hear her parking the car.

"She's getting out now."

I would listen in amazement as she described her mom's trajectory to our apartment. It seemed like my daughter was outside, following her mom's footsteps, and relaying to me what she was about to do.

"Mommy's close to the stairs… she's coming up… she's going to knock now…"

All of this before it actually happened! Before she learned to talk, many a time I'd see her staring fixed at a place near her, as though she was seeing something or someone. When she learned to articulate words and I asked her what was happening, she would say it was *o moço* (the guy) standing there. When she accumulated a larger vocabulary, she began talking about her other family in New York—a city she had never been to, and her brother named Jack—a name never mentioned in our Portuguese-speaking family, but that's another story.

Back to our adult/child NDE statistics, it is very likely that the adult 1 to 3 ratio is actually greater. Adults and children also have another peculiar difference—children are not as reserved as adults are to tell others about 'weird' things, as you may very well know if you have been around children long enough. It may take years for an adult NDEr to gather enough courage to tell others. The reason being that all too often, unfortunately, ridicule is the first reaction a NDEr receives when trying to tell somebody, even a spouse, about their extraordinary experience. Though they may be eager to share their incredible story, they keep it to themselves, until a good-hearted open-minded someone may stop and lend an ear.

In the beginning of the book your magical powers turned your inert doll into a lively little friend. You then helped it get out of its body; next, you yourself left your body and had a little taste of what it is like to live the spirit life. In that 'experience', you and your doll friend were in perfect health. Now you will have psychic vision, and will 'see' someone in the throes of death leaving the physical body, the first phase of a full-blown NDE. You will be witnessing immortality in the making.

Chapter 6

Witnessing Immortality

I was admitted to the hospital with heart trouble, and the next morning, lying in the hospital bed, I began to have a very severe pain in my chest. I pushed the button beside the bed to call the nurses, and they came in and started working on me. I was quite uncomfortable lying on my back so I turned over, and as I did I quit breathing and my heart stopped beating. Just then, I heard the nurses shout, "Code pink! Code pink!" As they were saying this, I could feel myself moving out of my body and sliding down between the mattress and the rail on the side of the bed—actually it seemed as if I went through the rail—on down to the floor. Then, I started rising upward, slowly. On my way up, I saw more nurses come running into the room—there must have been a dozen of them. My doctor happened to be making his rounds in the hospital so they called him and I saw him come in, too. I thought, 'I wonder what he's doing here.' I drifted on up past the light fixture—I saw it from the side and very distinctly—and then I stopped, floating right below the ceiling, looking down. I felt almost as though I were a piece of paper that someone had blown up to the ceiling.

I watched them reviving me from up there! My body was lying down there stretched out on the bed, in plain view, and they were all standing around it. I heard one say, "Oh, my God! She's gone!" while another one leaned down to give me mouth-to-mouth resuscitation. I was looking at the back of her head while she did this. I'll never forget the way her hair looked; it was cut kind of short. Just then, I saw them roll this machine in there, and they put the shocks on my chest. When they did, I saw my whole body just jump right up off the bed, and I heard every bone in my body crack and pop. It was the most awful thing!

As I saw them below beating on my chest and rubbing my arms and legs, I thought, 'Why are they going to so much trouble? I am just fine now.'[1]

You may have noticed by this account what I mean when I say that our consciousness is not locked up in the brain like a bird in a cage. When this lady was physically conscious her locus of consciousness was in her physical head, indeed manifested through the brain. However, as the heart and the brain quit their normal functioning, her consciousness along with her spirit body slipped out, intact, and continued their independent existence, without the need of—in fact, better without!—a physical apparatus.

If you had been one of those attending nurses and had psychic vision, this is what you would have seen when the woman turned to her side, stopped breathing, and felt herself leaving the body. Around the head, you would see a mist-like substance gathering, shapeless at first, and then coming into form. In a few seconds, you would have seen the shape of a new head—face, eyes, nose and all! This was the moment when the woman said, "I could feel myself moving out of my body." Seconds later, astounded and with your jaws dropping again, you would have seen an entire new body exiting the physical counterpart. You would have seen it sliding down between the mattress and the rail—metal rail, for that matter—moving out with ease and grace and in the most absolute freedom as material objects were no longer barriers to the spirit body. No longer bound by the law of gravity, rather than forcibly pulled to the center of the earth, as a physical body would be, it rose up, lightly and gently, as a delicate feather floating in a soft breeze.

At this moment, something would draw your attention. As you stared at the spirit body floating above you, you would see a remarkable resemblance to the physical counterpart, with some enhancements. You would see, for example, smoother skin, a younger looking face, brighter perfect teeth, and a suppler constitution to name a few visible differences. She could have emerged to the non-physical reality dressed in a similar garment as the physical body she was leaving, but of a finer, silk-like material, or the same way, as a baby, she emerged to the physical world—naked as a jaybird. But regardless of what covered the new body, if anything, you would be certain it had a connection to the body lying dead on the hospital bed. Somehow, they were related. If a departed loved one were to appear to you, this is how you would recognize her or him—by the appearance of their last earthly incarnation, one that you would recognize.

As you glanced between the two bodies to make further comparisons, you would notice something you had seen before, but thicker now. You would see, connecting both bodies, a rope-like energy cord—the silver cord—attached to the forehead, throat or stomach of the physical body, and to the back of the head of the spirit body. Paying closer attention to the cord, you could tell it was not static. It seemed to pulsate as energy from the spirit body ran to the physical to keep it whole.

When I asked Celi to tell me what she had seen in the ICU while out of her body, there was more than the body lying in bed with tubes and cables connected to monitors. In fact, she caught me by surprise. Asking about it had not even crossed my mind, since it is something nearly unheard of in NDE accounts, with rare exceptions.

"What else drew your attention?" I asked.

"The cord," she replied.

Since this was precious information, I pretended I did not know what she was referring to.

"On the monitors?"

"No, there was a cord attached to the body that came to my direction. To the back of my head, I think."

"How was this cord?"

"Like a rope, sort of."

"Was there a color to it?"

"Silverish like."

Since our floating woman had not moved too far out, and if you as a nurse would go back in time to assist the physical birth of this person, you would see that the silver cord resembled the baby's umbilical cord. And this would take you to a startling conclusion—death and birth are similar events with opposing destinations. The child whose birth you had assisted hailed from the spirit world and through her mother grew a physical body to experiment life on earth. When her job on earth was done, as you witnessed the death of her physical body, you saw the spirit body emerge from the physical—umbilical cord and all—to return to the spiritual dimension again, our true home. You might have heard or read or even told your friends the famous quote by Pierre Teilhard de Chardin—*we are not human beings having a spiritual experience, but spiritual beings having a human experience*—now you know what he meant.

If the floating lady had not been too concerned about watching what was happening to her physical body down below, and was aware that she could fly anywhere she wanted just by thinking of it, this is what you would have seen happening to her silver cord. You would see it stretch and thin, and the farther she went the thinner the cord became. If she were far away, you would see the cord as thin as or even thinner than a hair shaft or a spider web thread. She could go to the other side of this universe or to another universe and the cord would not snap! The silver cord snaps only when the body dies. And the body dies when it is ready to die, when the spirit's earthly mission is done.

Knowing that as long as the cord is connected the physical body is alive, you as a psychic nurse could have an interesting time watching your colleagues. As long as you could see the cord you knew there was vital life to the body, therefore it could be revived.

"She's gone!" a colleague would say.

"No, she's not!" you would reply. "Keep trying! She'll come around."

On the other hand, if you saw the cord snap and your colleague said, "Let's keep going, we'll bring her back!"

You would then say, "No use, she's gone!"

Our woman, who had ventured away for a moment, must return because her time on earth was not over yet. You would then see the cord thickening as she approached the physical body, back to the thickness of the umbilical cord as she was a couple of yards away. You would then see the cord, like a bungee rope, pulling her spirit body fast into the physical. Whereas just a moment ago you were seeing two bodies, one in bed and the other out, now both had—in astral travel lingo—coincided, thus you would see only the physical. At this very moment you could anticipate what your colleagues, still working frantically to revive the body, would say next.

"Oh my God! She's back! We got a heartbeat!"

As you would visit this patient later to check up on her or bring her medicine, having seen what had happened, you would hint if she wanted to comment about the time she had a cardiac arrest... She would eagerly leap to the opportunity, and the more you showed understanding and interest, the more she would tell you. If she had had a full-blown NDE, she would tell you some amazing things waiting for us when it is our turn to kiss earth goodbye. Some of them you are about to see; just turn the page.

Chapter 7

The Ten Phases of NDE

NDEs around the world follow a basic pattern. Ten common phases can be observed in a *full-blown* NDE. However, not all NDErs experience all the phases, and some may experience a particular phase or phases not included in the ten basic ones. For instance, rather than entering a tunnel and arriving at a heavenly place, the person leaves the physical body and goes to the hospital waiting room to comfort relatives, or back home, or for a *floating* stroll to a park, or just hangs outside the hospital, then returns to physical life.

Here are the ten phases:

1. Sensation of leaving the physical body, OBE
2. Feeling of peace and well-being
3. Seeing what's happening
4. In the darkness
5. A light in the darkness
6. In the spirit world
7. A barrier in the beyond
8. Life review and the Being of Light
9. Back to the physical body
10. Life change

Phase 1: Sensation of Leaving the Physical Body

With this phase you're already quite familiar; you not only just 'heard' the woman telling about it, but also 'saw' it happening. One thing she did not mention and that could happen when the spirit body is exiting the physical is hearing some internal noises. It is normal to hear snapping sounds throughout the body, like when you crumple cellophane wrap; as the spirit force accumulates in the head, whooshing, buzzing or ringing sounds are common, and a *pop* may be heard at the moment the spirit body frees itself and exits the physical counterpart. I have had such experiences a few times as I consciously worked my way out of the body during OBEs. Another possibility is a brief loss of consciousness at the moment the spirit body exits the physical, and rather than feeling the entire exiting process, like our lady did, the person would find herself or himself already out of the body somewhere without knowing exactly how it happened.

You also noticed that during this phase the person, separated from the physical body, is capable of thinking, seeing, hearing, talking—and all this is done from the new body's perspective—not from the physical, which in a great number of cases is clinically dead. In this phase, the person may also realize that she or he still has a body and discovers, for the first time, her or his immortality. And this realization may cause the NDEr to care less for the physical body being revived. She or he just discovered that death is not the end and is thrilled about it.

I spend a great part of my life researching, lecturing, and writing about our spirituality, death, dying, and the afterlife—including books in my native Portuguese—for two reasons. One is to re-familiarize the listener and reader with their immortality. I say re-familiarize because intuitively they know it, but the struggle for physical survival on the earth plane is so great that many lose focus on their spiritual side. The other is to 're-educate' them for that not so mysterious moment when their earthly work is done and the time comes to discard the physical body to return to the spiritual home. One thing I tell you, do not fear death, you will continue to exist.

Phase 2: Feeling of Peace and Well-Being

Life on earth is a boot camp for the soul, and the physical body the equipment we use to do the exercises we signed up for. As every other equipment, though much more sophisticated, of course, eventually the body wears out, quite painfully, at times. The physical body is to us, spirit that we really are, what a caterpillar is to the butterfly or the shell to a turtle—a necessary but a heavy burden to carry.

Once free from the bounds of matter, the person going through a NDE, as we have already seen, may enjoy an ineffable feeling of peace and well-being. Having also just recognized that life goes on, the NDEr, who until then might have been afraid of dying, may lose the fear of death completely, or have it drastically reduced.

A Brazilian man I will call Antonio was attending one of my lectures on *Emancipation of the Soul During NDE*, as I entitle it, in a Spiritist center in South Florida. I have learned to identify NDErs during my lectures by the look in their faces as I detail the experience. When they are close enough I can even see tears welling up in their eyes. Antonio had been nodding from start to finish, and his eyes did tear up. So I knew he had had one. And certainty came when he approached me at the end.

I also have learned from my own experiences that God indeed has mysterious—and often quite effective—ways of setting us back on track when we stray too far from the spiritual path. Antonio's was his NDE. Antonio did not recall leaving his body or floating upwards as in other accounts. When he became conscious again he found himself out of his body. His NDE occurred during a cardiac arrest. Here is what he told me about Phase Two:

I was feeling a discomfort in my chest, and it kept increasing. The pain and pressure were so great that I felt like fainting. Then the strangest thing happened. The pain was gone completely, and I noticed I wasn't in my body anymore. I was surrounded by the most beautiful sounds, like some kind of celestial music. The harmony is impossible to describe. You'd have to hear it to understand what I mean. I then noticed the light; I was immersed in a radiant light. Something I'd never seen or believed existed. All my life I had lived by the clock— meetings, lunch and dinner appointments, but there time had lost its meaning. The next thing that drew my attention was how well I was feeling. The lightness, the peace, the joy were unfathomable. It was like finding my own essence or the essence of everything. I could stay there forever.

Wiping a tear rolling down his cheek, Antonio repeated a phrase that you hear again and again when talking to a NDEr who had a positive experience, "This is as close as I can get in describing it with words. It is something you can never forget."

Though most NDEs can be considered positive, Antonio's being a very intense one, there are those which are the extreme opposite. Rather than experiencing such heightened feelings, the NDEr goes through a phase of mental agony, especially when caused by suicide attempt and drug overdose, as we will see in chapters 11, 12 and 13.

Phase 3: Seeing What Is Happening

This is the phase that can be considered the rock in the shoe of conventional scientists. It is also the phase in which the veracity of what some researchers call the *continuity of consciousness*— remember, they cannot say *spirit*—after bodily death can be verified. You've seen this phase in the account of the floating woman whose NDE you witnessed with your psychic vision.

As I have already mentioned, a great number of NDEs occur when the patient is clinically dead. Note that in clinical death the patient is unconscious, the heart is not beating, and the brain is not receiving oxygen and does not register activity. Therefore, the occipital lobe, an area in the back of the brain responsible for receiving and processing visual information, is inactive. And even if it were active, it would not produce any visual information because the eyes of an unconscious patient are, needless to say, tightly shut. Therefore, they are not capturing any image for the occipital lobe to process. However, even in this extremely torpid state many NDErs see what's going on around, or—as in most cases—below them.

Scared to Death in the Morgue

I was in Crumpsall Hospital near Manchester... I can still picture the scene. I saw myself lying on the bed. I saw a young nurse. She was preparing me for mortuary. I remember thinking at the time how young she was to have to do such a thing as getting me ready and even shaving me. I actually saw it taking place. I was detached from it, it was as if I was there watching and I was a third party. I felt no emotion, just nothing, like looking at a picture. I was clinically dead about two hours. I woke up at the mortuary of Crumpsall Hospital and it was the mortuary attendant who nearly had a heart attack! I know it wasn't a dream.[1]

You have already noticed and will notice repeatedly that when NDErs report seeing what is happening around or below them, they see it from a perspective away from the physical body. The locus of consciousness moves from the physical body to the new body, and it is no longer brain-based, since the brain may not even be working at all. This shift of consciousness from the physical brain to the non-physical body is the most eloquent indicator that consciousness is not a by-product—or an epiphenomenon, as erudite scientists like to call it—of the brain, and it can and does operate without it.

In NDE research, there are two camps of scientists: one camp that wants to prove that consciousness can continue after bodily death, and the other working to debunk the notion. The ones for continuity would make efforts to verify the information given by the NDErs, while the ones against it would not even bother to hear of it. The debunkers come up with reductionist justifications such as dreams, hallucinations, or fantasies the brain creates to reduce our innate fear of death, and so on, not taking into consideration that a clinically dead brain cannot produce dreams, hallucinations, or neuronal fantasies. Moreover, they should know it better than anyone else. Are they not brain scientists?

Phase 4: In the Darkness

In the previous phases—with the exception of Antonio's—you noticed that NDErs were around the physical body, in the physical environment. Hence their ability to see medical personnel, equipment and procedures being utilized to revive the body; and they could also clearly hear conversations going on. In summary, they remained on earth's physical dimension. Prior to beginning their entrance in the spiritual or non-physical dimension, many NDErs report a brief period when they find themselves immersed in intense darkness.

Here we will revisit my cousin Celi's NDE experience. As I continued our interview, I asked:

"Did you stay in the ICU the whole time?"

"No," she answered, "I went out sometimes."

"Around the hospital?"

"No, outside."

"Like in the city?"

"No, somewhere else."

"Could you explain?

"The first time I felt thirsty, so I walked out of the room looking for water."

You may be wondering if she were in her spirit body, how she could feel thirsty. When we are still connected to the physical body, or even in cases of recent physical death, we can still carry strong impressions of the physical life, like feeling thirsty, hungry, cold, pain, or even projecting wounds on the spirit body. I have, during several OBEs, instructed recent discarnate individuals carrying such impressions that they were not real, since the nature of their new bodies had changed.

"Where did you go?" I asked Celi.

"I do not know exactly. First everything was dark, darkness everywhere..."

Celi then experienced the next phase, she continued...

Phase 5: A Light in the Darkness

"... I turned around to go back and a tiny bright light caught my attention. I stared at it and felt like I was supposed to follow it, so I did. I am not sure if I walked toward the light or the light came toward me. But it would expand as I approached it. It was very intense and peaceful. Then the darkness disappeared and I was in a green meadow filled with people in white."

"Did you recognize anyone?"

"No."

"Did you mingle with them?"

"No. I'd stay there a while then would find myself back in the hospital."

"Did you go there only once?"

"No, other times too."

Celi did not mention this, but many NDErs are afraid the intense light might hurt their eyes. Such concern is also a sign of the strong connection with the physical body. And they feel surprised when they look straight at it and no damage is done.

Phase 6: In the Realm of Spirits

We have not seen it in the previous cases, but the point of light may expand and open up into a tunnel, through which NDErs travel, stopping upon reaching a spiritual place. An interesting aspect of the previous two phases, darkness and the light in the darkness (and the tunnel), is that they always lead to a realm identified as spiritual. Once there, NDErs may meet discarnate relatives or friends or other spiritual beings they may not recognize. It is as though this darkness is some kind of barrier between the physical and the spiritual realms, and the point of light a passage leading to the land of spirits.

In all the cases I have known personally and in all scholarly papers and books I have read on NDE—tons of them—I have never found a researcher reporting a peculiar thing. You never hear NDErs say that they entered the darkness, saw a point of bright light, followed it, or traveled through a tunnel, and found themselves in, for example, Hackensack, New Jersey, or in a brighter place if they have been good, like our sunny South Beach here in Miami, or any other physical city, where they met Aunt Sally, or Grandpa Moses, both still physically alive.

No! It is always the same sequence—darkness, bright light, tunnel, spiritual realm, discarnate beings, regardless of where the NDE is occurring. And this is strong evidence that NDE is a spiritual occurrence taking place outside the brain and outside physical dimension. Again, a flatlined, shutdown brain cannot produce the slowest wave, let alone such spectacular experiences, as we will shortly see.

The green meadow my cousin Celi found herself in after the light is a common feature in NDE accounts. The case below is an example. However, Celi's experience was not as dramatic as this woman's was after having a cardiac arrest under anesthetic.

A Taste of Heaven

Then I found myself, I was in a beautiful landscape, the grass is greener than anything seen on earth, it has special light or glow. The colors are beyond description, the colors here are so drab by comparison. The light is brighter than anything possible to imagine. There are no words to describe it; it is a heavenly light. In this place, I saw people that I knew had died. There were no words spoken, but it was as if I knew what they were thinking and at the same time, I knew that they knew what I was thinking. I felt a peace that passed all understanding. It was a marvelous feeling. I felt exhilarated and felt I was one with everything. I saw Christ but the light coming from Him was so bright that it would normally blind you. I felt as if I wanted to stay there forever, but someone, I felt it was my guardian angel, said, "You have to go back as you haven't finished your term." Then I felt a kind of vibrating and I was back again.[2]

This "vibrating" you may have already experienced yourself, even if you have never had a NDE. In OBE or astral projection lingo, it is called *vibrational state*, as I have mentioned earlier in my own experience. I also commented it is a typical feeling prior to an OBE, as the spirit body begins its separation from the physical, and common as well when the spirit body returns to or coincides with the physical after a short 'discarnate' sojourn, either in the spiritual or physical dimensions. The vibrational state most commonly occurs during sleep, but one can learn to induce it during relaxation as preparation for a conscious OBE. However, it is not necessary to reach the vibrational state in order to leave the body; it can happen without it, as is most often the case.

Phase 7: A Barrier in the Beyond

This phase presents a peculiar paradox. Many NDErs—in fact, most of humanity—may have been scared of dying. Then they have a NDE and see that death is far from being the fearful monster they thought it was. They find themselves in a spiritual land, surrounded by beauty and loved ones they thought were gone forever, and hit a barrier that, if crossed, they will not return to physical life. And they are tempted to cross it, even knowing that their earthly life would be history. The barrier can be tangible or intangible, or rather than seeing it NDErs sense that if they go beyond a certain point they will stay. And here is the paradox.

Before they knew what death really meant they were scared and did not want to die, now they know that they will not die, they want to stay (physically) *dead*.

In most cases the barrier is tangible and visible, represented by a river, a stream, a ravine, a gate or...

A Heavenly Fence

I 'died' from a cardiac arrest, and, as I did, I suddenly found myself in a rolling field. It was beautiful, and everything was of intense green—a color unlike anything on earth. There was light—beautiful, uplifting light—all around me. I looked ahead of me, across the field, and I saw a fence. I started moving towards the fence, and I saw a man on the other side of it, moving towards it as to meet me. I wanted to reach him, but I felt myself drawn back, irresistibly. As I did, I saw him too turn around and go back in the other direction, away from the fence.[3]

Phase 8: Life Review and the Being of Light

The review of one's life seems a common practice humans engage in when the end of physical life is approaching, and not only when they are having a NDE. In my experience working with dying patients as a hospice volunteer, I heard it many times. When I asked if they were happy with the outcome of the review, the answer was normally no, or if not entirely negative, it was not entirely positive either. When I asked if they would change anything if given another chance, the answer was yes, and when I asked what they would change, the answer was many things, if not everything.

This phase can be a good lesson for us while we wait our time to return to our spiritual home. Knowing that we will have to give account of our actions somehow when crossing to the other side of life—perhaps to our own consciousness, which is even worse—we could start the review now and fix what needs to be fixed beforehand. I have learned from the dying that grudges, hatreds, unforgiveness, and all sorts of unfinished business are terrible deterrents to a peaceful passage. As we have already seen and will see more later on, death of the physical body will not erase the memories of who we are and what we have done. Both in this life and in the next, the quality of our thoughts, emotions, and actions and the ensuing consequences they inevitably bring dictate the state of our mind and of our life. It will be, here or there, heavenly or hellish, according to how we spend our precious time and energy in the eternal journey of spiritual evolution. Our destiny is in our own hands, and in our hands is also the power to change it from sour to sweet, if we so desire. In the words of Francisco Xavier, not only Brazil's greatest medium but perhaps the greatest humanitarian of our nation, *we cannot change our past, but we can start now and change our future.*

The life review NDErs go through, in earth time, takes just a few seconds. It is an intense and detailed reliving of their actions up to that moment in their lives, in panoramic view in many occasions. Normally they see or feel a presence they generally term a *Being of Light* who guides them in the process, with love and compassion but no judgment. NDErs may feel ashamed and remorseful of their mistakes, especially when they have hurt others, worse when the others are loved ones such as spouse, parents, and children. During the life review, NDErs report they not only see their actions, but feel deep in their own being the pain and sorrow they caused, as though they were the ones being hurt. What they learn in this phase prompts them to make changes once they are back to physical life.

Dying to Learn

During a NDE caused by a nearly fatal fall, a man who had a life review accompanied by a Being of Light reported the following experience:

My life started to flash before me. I felt embarrassed every time a stupid thing I had done came up. I sensed that the 'presence' was saying, "Yes, you did these things, but you were learning at the same time." It was then communicated to me that I should go back. I did not want to, but I understood that there was still a lot of work for me to do.[4]

Phase 9: Return to the Body

This is another paradoxical moment of a NDE. Ask anyone if they want to die. The word *death* is taboo around the planet; nobody wants to even think about it, let alone dying. When someone is diagnosed with a terminal illness, the first reaction is denial (as the first stage identified by the late Dr. Elisabeth Kübler-Ross), and despair may set in for a while. Tons of money may be spent trying to dodge the Grim Reaper's deadly scythe. Then a person has a NDE and gets a glimpse of life in the beyond, and is told or feels that it is time to return to the physical body to resume earthly life, but the person does not want to—she or he wants to stay *dead*! With the exception of NDE by suicide attempt or overdose during which the NDEr might recognize the mistake and want to return to earthly life to make amends, the great majority of NDErs having a positive experience want to stay in the beyond.

Returning by Force

Pam Reynolds, whose extraordinary experience we will see in detail in Chapter 9, had a NDE during a very difficult surgical procedure. After going through the phases we have seen above, Pam saw her deceased grandmother beackoning her to approach. Other deceased relatives were present as well. At a certain moment Pam was told she had to return, since it was not her time yet. A deceased uncle accompanied Pam back to the hospital. Upon seeing her body on the operating table, Pam was terrified and refused to enter it. So reluctant was she to get back into the body that the dead uncle had to push her inside.[5]

Phase 10: A Change of Life

It is common for NDErs to report that they see themselves in the presence of the Being of Light (recognized by some Christians as Jesus), and are asked: *What have you done with your life that's worth showing me?* Such a question, especially to those whose life has not been so nobly spent, has a painful yet illuminating effect at times. Painful because they feel in the core of their being the remorse of the evil done to another human being, and illuminating because they discover the true reason of their earthly existence—to learn to love and to acquire knowledge. Emmanuel, through the mediumship of Francisco Xavier, wrote that love and knowledge are the two wings which will fly us to infinite perfection.[6] And NDErs seem to corroborate this statement.

Once back to the physical life to continue their lessons in the great school earth is, the majority of NDErs change their way of life radically. First, they lose their fear of death entirely, or see it drastically reduced. Towards the end of my interview with my cousin Celi, I asked if she was afraid to die. "Not a bit," she replied. "Life goes on," she added.

Another positive change is their becoming more loving towards people, as they discover the great brotherhood humanity is, accepting others—and themselves—the way they are. Materialism may lose its fascination, and time and energy are put to greater service, such as in volunteer work to benefit others. Earthly life is now seen as a divine gift to be appreciated every minute. The need to acquire knowledge becomes urgent, and many return to school. Many cases of discovering hidden artistic talents have been reported or even spontaneous developments of psychic gifts such as clairvoyance or healing touch.

The positive effects resulting from NDEs has prompted British doctor Sam Parnia, currently one of the most active NDE researchers, to speak out about the importance of mapping areas of the brain involved in 'producing' NDE. Why does he think such mapping is so important? In his materialistic medical view, to develop medications to stimulate those areas in order to recreate the positive effects of a NDE, thus treating psychological and psychiatric conditions.[7]

Here you might be wondering as I did when I read it. If in many cases the brain shows no activity, being even *flatlined* at times, no part of the brain had been activated by the NDE. Therefore, no medication will be capable of bringing about the positive effects of a NDE. What produces NDE is not the activity of the brain or the body. The extreme opposite is true. It is its inactivity. To consciously induce an OBE, for instance, the first thing to be done is the reduction of both physical and mental activities. And once the spirit body leaves the physical, consciousness is immediately transferred to the spirit body and the physical body becomes cataleptic or paralyzed. During a NDE the opposite occurs. The body becomes torpid, and the brain inactive because of a certain condition, which makes it much easier for a person—as spirit she or he really is—to leave the body momentarily, or permanently, if the earthly work is done.

But if Sam Parnia, an experienced and respected medical doctor and NDE researcher as he is, knows that in many cases there is no brain activity, why would he make such a suggestion? Because to him, like to other researchers who do not believe in the existence of a surviving soul or spirit, NDE—a neuronal fantasy, in this case—occurs prior to the cessation of brain activity or after brain function returns to normal. Never during the loss of consciousness. Why do not they believe that NDE occurs during the period of clinical death or unconsciousness?

Here we find another paradox, a catch-22, in the words of Joseph Heller. Because there is no brain activity! And without brain activity—to them—a human being ceases to exist!

However, cases upon cases of NDEs have shown and

continue to show that, as we would say in Brazil, *the hole is farther down*; things may not be as we think they are. Tightly chained to deep-rooted preconceived ideas and unwilling to shift paradigms, or at least granting the benefit of doubt, materialistic scientists concoct reductionist explanations to account for NDEs. Any theory may be valid which excludes the possibility of the existence of an immaterial element in a human being that is capable of living independently of the brain.

If materialistic science is correct, why are so many NDErs able to feel, see, hear, think and mentally record events during the period they are clinically dead and unconscious? And later, upon being resuscitated, are able to recall in minute details events that took place during that time?

This may be the reason...

Chapter 8

Brain Not Required

If you are a Johnny Depp fan as I am, you must have seen *Dark Shadows*. His character, the flamboyant vampire Barnabas Collins, is disinterred in 1972. Things have changed quite a bit since he went underground 200 years before. When Barnabas sees a TV for the first time, Karen Carpenter singing The Carpenters' 1972 hit song *Top of the World*, he attacks the tube. "What sorcery is this?" Pulling the power cord, he demands, "Reveal yourself, tiny songstress!"

As you know too well, Barnabas could have taken the TV set apart, bit by tiny bit, and all that he would find would be screws, wires, valves and transistors, and no tiny songstress or anything coming up next would reveal itself. Why would it not? Because a TV set is a specialized equipment, designed to capture, decode and display visual images and sound waves whose signals are dispersed throughout space. A TV set does not produce nor store such signals. As you turn on a TV set on a certain channel, it receives, decodes, and transmits images and sounds attuned to that frequency; images which are floating freely throughout space and whose source is elsewhere. As you turn off the set, you cannot see the signals anymore, but they continue to exist.

Barnabas could have smashed the TV set to smithereens but the tiny songstress would keep on singing somewhere! He would not see it, of course, since he would have destroyed the device through which the image was manifested, but the image would not be destroyed. The image and the sound were independent from the device created to manifest them.

As far as consciousness—or spirit—is concerned, this analogy can be usefully applied to understand the brain/consciousness relationship. The brain and its component parts—brain stem, cortex, cerebellum, hippocampus, thalamus, hypothalamus, pituitary and pineal glands, neurons etc—produce, store, and transmit physical elements such as hormones and neurotransmitters. And just as a TV set does not produce or store images and sounds, the brain does not produce or store consciousness. It simply processes consciousness while we are focused on physical reality.

Neuroscientists in many countries are spending countless hours in state-of-the-art labs and investing immense amounts of money on sophisticated equipment to study the brain. Consciousness researchers in these labs are endeavoring to locate the area in the brain which produces consciousness—this elusive part of us which accounts for our personality, our character, our morality, our humanity, our virtues, our knowledge, our talents, our goodness, our capacity to love or to hate, our wickedness and our emotions etc. Will they ever find consciousness inside the brain? They will find consciousness inside the brain when Barnabas finds the tiny songstress inside the tube. And just as the tiny songstress would survive the demise of the tube, consciousness, likewise, will survive the demise of the physical brain—because it is not there.

So…

Where in the *Bleep* is Consciousness?

"Three regions figure repeatedly and prominently in studies of mechanisms related to attention, neglect and consciousness, namely the posterior parietal cortex, the prefrontal cortex and a medial territory centered on the cingulate gyrus."[1] And these three regions are part of the cerebral cortex. If you ask a neuroscientist where exactly in the brain consciousness is located or produced, he will say he does not know or is not sure, or might suggest a certain place. But if you ask him about a general area, he would not hesitate to say somewhere in the cerebral cortex, or the gray matter, as you remember from your anatomy class.

"Why is that?" you would ask him.

"Because," he would answer, "in the cerebral cortex there are areas involved in activities such as speech, hearing, vision, thought, dreaming, perception, learning, emotions, problem solving, motor, sensory, memory—thus your ability to remember your anatomy class—all of which are associated with consciousness."[2]

Suppose your curious eight-year-old child had tagged along and was snooping on your conversation with the neuroscientist, and she heard a teacher say that there was no such thing as a stupid question.

"What if a person doesn't have a cortex?" your child would blurt out.

You might feel embarrassed as you see the neuroscientist frown. But you already know the answer. He had just told you that the cortex is responsible for activities such as speech, hearing, vision, memory, thought, dreaming, perception, learning, emotions, problem solving, motor, sensory, all associated with consciousness, thus no cortex, no such activities, and no consciousness, right?

Not quite!

Anencephaly, from the Greek 'no brain', is a birth defect characterized by the absence of "the front part of the brain (forebrain) and the thinking and coordinating part of the brain (cerebrum). The remaining parts of the brain are often not covered by bone or skin. In the US alone in every 4,850 or so births one baby is born with some degree of anencephaly."[3]

Now suppose your child decided to expand on the question. On first hearing it, you might be tempted to report to the principal the teacher who said there was no such thing as a stupid question. "What if rather than having a cortex, a person had water in their head, would they have consciousness, vision, emotions, perception?"

Can you picture the expression on the neuroscientist's face? If he had frowned on the question of having no cortex, he'd certainly display facial contortions on this one. But your child knew what she was getting at.

Within anencephaly there is a rare condition termed hydranencephaly. By the Greek prefix *hydra* you guessed where we are headed—water! In hydranencephaly, instead of having a cortex the brain's cerebral hemispheres (where the three regions responsible for consciousness are supposed to be located) are absent and replaced by sacs filled with cerebrospinal fluid."[4]

Bjorn Merker, a Swedish neuroscientist with a PhD in brain science and psychology from Massachusetts Institute of Technology (MIT), studied several children with hydranencephaly. In a paper entitled "Consciousness without a Cerebral Cortex: A challenge for neuroscience and medicine" (2007), he wrote about his observations, "These children are not only awake and often alert, but show responsiveness to their surroundings in the form of emotional or orienting reactions to environmental events. They express pleasure by smiling and laughter, and aversion by 'fussing', arching of the back and crying, their faces being animated by these emotional states."[5]

There was a highly publicized case in Brazil of Vitoria de Cristo (Victory of Christ), born in January 2010 and surviving (physically) until July 2012. Her parents went public against early pregnancy termination of anencephalic babies, and had this to say about their daughter, "Everybody says that everything she does is just reflexes, but we've always questioned it because she smiles, grimaces when getting a shot, tries to communicate, shows satisfaction and discomfort."[6]

Academically, Merker was not the only neuroscientist to study anencephalic or hydranencephalic children. In 1999 pediatric neurologist, Dr. Alan Shewmon and colleagues investigated "four children ages 5 to 17, with congenital brain malformations involving total or nearly total absence of cerebral cortex...

According to traditional neurophysiologic theory, consciousness requires neocortical functioning (a whole and fully working cortex), and children born without cerebral hemispheres necessarily remain indefinitely in a developmental vegetative state."[7] But this was not what Merker and Shewmon found out in the children they investigated, or what Vitoria's parents witnessed in her behavior during the two and half years they cared for their beloved child.

Perhaps the most important lesson these children taught Merker and Shewmon was that *traditional neurophysiologic theory of consciousness* must be revised—and urgently! For even without a cerebral cortex these children were able to differentiate familiar and unfamiliar people and places, showed social interaction, musical preference, associative learning, appropriate affective responses, and functional vision orienting.[8] According to traditional theory of consciousness this could not have happened because these children lacked a cerebral cortex, which, in its view, is the producer of consciousness. But defying this traditional view some level of consciousness was present in these children despite the lack of a cortex, which clearly shows that consciousness is not produced by the brain.

Now, in order to have vision at any level, we need more than just a set of healthy eyes. We need a healthy occipital lobe, so says traditional neurophysiology. "Visual information transmitted from the eye is first processed in the occipital lobe (located in the posterior part of the cortex). Impulses from the retina of both eyes arrive in this part of the cortex,"[9] thus enabling us to see. We also learn from neuroscience that "damage to the visual cortex, which is located on the surface of the occipital lobe, can cause blindness due to the holes in the visual map."[10]

Suppose the neuroscientist you were talking to—who had nearly foamed at the mouth at your child's question of water in the brain—ended up taking a liking to your child and was calmly explaining to her about this occipital lobe thing. But for some reason your child was determined to get on the scientist's nerves, and asked, "What if people are born without an occipital lobe? Or the visual cortex, could not they see anyways?"

Now this question might have been the last straw on their would-be friendship, but, again, your child knew why she was asking it. There is a saying in my country that goes something like this: In the land of the blind, whoever has one eye is king.

Suppose two persons do not have healthy occipital lobes and visual cortex, but do have a tiny rudimentary part of them; and two others lack them completely, not a sliver of either. Even if we are not brain scientists, traditional or otherwise, we would not hesitate to believe that the two persons with at least a tiny fragment should be king over the two with no visual cortex at all. If one of the groups were to have vision, or defying traditional neurophysiology, if both groups were to have vision, the group with vision or better vision must be the one with at least a hint of visual cortex, not the other which lacks it completely. This seems a logical conclusion. But this was not what Dr. Shewmon and his colleagues discovered. "Ironically, they (with no visual cortex) possessed the most vision despite total lack of occipital cortex, in contrast to the other two, who had little or no vision despite occipital remnants."[11]

And just here is plenty of reason why the current traditional consciousness as a by-product of the brain paradigm must be revaluated.

Though the children investigated by Dr. Shewmon were aged five to seventeen, anencephalic or hydranencephalic babies rarely survive too long. "If the infant is not stillborn, then he or she will usually die within a few hours or days after birth."[12] But despite such a poor prognosis there are many cases of children surviving past age three, but not much longer. But why such a short life span if many have shown active consciousness and vision despite the absence of a brain?

Because the body—*the body*—needs a brain to survive. "The brain controls all of our internal processes, such as the beating of our heart, the digestion of our food, and the rate of our breathing, without us having to even think about it."[13] The survival of the physical body, the material apparatus we, as spirit, are using to experience life on earth, depends on the works of a fully operating brain to experience a fully healthy physical life. When out of our body we can think, talk, hear, smell, feel, and move without the need of a brain, but when we are focused on the physical body it is the brain that co-ordinates these activities, as well as others responsible for maintaining the organic force that keeps the body alive.

The fact that consciousness was present in anencephalic and hydranencephalic children lacking a cerebral cortex shows that consciousness is not a by-product of the brain or brain processes, as traditional neurophysiology postulates. Consciousness is simply manifested through the brain while we are focused on the physical body. The reason for the limited manifestation of consciousness in anencephalic and hydranencephalic children is not that their consciousness is not 'whole', which it is, but because the brain is defective, too incomplete to allow full and unrestrained manifestation of it.

If Barnabas Collins' TV set had been defective when he saw it for the first time, he would not see the tiny songstress in her entirety. He would see her image imperfect and distorted. If the speaker was malfunctioning, her voice could break up or sound squeaky, stammering or mute. However, the *defect* by no means was in the image being manifested, but in the apparatus through which it was being manifested. The image, a non-physical entity, having its origin elsewhere, independently created, and present everywhere at the same time, was whole and complete. It had a life of its own but when seen in association with a TV set—like consciousness and the brain— it gave the illusion that it was an inherent part or a by-product of the set; but it was not.

When we are awake and active, we are like a TV set turned on, fully manifested in the physical body and brain. But when the physical body is 'turned off', such as during NDE or OBE, our consciousness—or spirit—retreats temporarily, but does not cease to exist. And it will not cease to exist by the death of the body.

Love Lessons

If you, with your psychic vision, happened to be present when one of those children was leaving physical life, you would marvel at the sight. You would see rising out of that incomplete physical body a whole spirit body—perfect and fully alive. As she or he turned to you, flashing a beautiful smile of relief for the end of such a trying experience, you could ask: "Why are you leaving so soon? What have you come here to learn?"

"This time," you would hear as an answer, "I came to teach, not to learn."

Teach what? you might think to yourself, wondering how she or he could have taught anything to anybody in such sorry physical condition in such a short time.

The child, now a little angel floating freely and gracefully in front of you, whole and unhindered, no longer encumbered by the limitations of that physical body, picked up your thought. That simple answer coming out of her or his now fully perfect mind, showed its power on that now even more radiant face.

"Love! I came to teach love and my job is done. I'm heading home now."

In the previous chapter, we saw that one of the main lessons NDErs discover they are supposed to learn on earth is the need to love. And our loving God has some mysterious ways to make us learn this precious lesson. When you read or hear what families of children with anencephaly tell about the lessons learned from their angels in disguise, it is all about love. The grandmother of a Colorado boy, who lived three years without a brain, could not be any clearer about it. "[He] taught his family how to love and about the strength of family... He was our hero because he showed the strength if I can do this anything can be done."[14]

In the heart-warming, tear-shedding BlogSpot Vitoria's parents set up in her memory, they wrote, "Love overcomes fear and makes us free to be happy. Vitoria taught us to love, to be free and to find joy in small things. Through this precious child, we learned what love really is and what it is to be truly happy."[15] Contagious as it is, love transcends boundaries—no distance is unreachable and no heart is impermeable to the great healing force God breathes onto His creation in strange ways. Vitoria, one of these God-sent messengers, taught lessons of love not only to her family, but also to many others who heard her story, in the most distant parts of the world. Someone wrote this beautiful message the day Vitoria returned to the heavenly home she had hailed from: "Beautiful little angel, today Heaven is celebrating the return of its newest and distinguished resident, your mission here on earth was fulfilled with honor, you and your parents taught us the true meaning of the word LOVE."[16] (Capitalized by the writer of the message.)

From these special children we learn that consciousness may not need a fully operating brain to manifest itself in physical life. From NDErs we go a step further—we learn that not only is a brain not required for the manifestation of consciousness, but also it can live independently of it. Thus, even out of the body a person's identity remains intact; nothing is impaired, nothing is lost. Moreover, repeatedly NDErs give us testimony that the death of the body does not extinguish consciousness. On the contrary, it releases consciousness and allows it greater freedom and the ability to transcend dimensions.

The following is an extraordinary account that adds strength to the consciousness survival hypothesis sponsored by the camp researching NDE to prove that life goes on after bodily death. Come along and see for yourself the greatness that life is; the greatness that we are.

Chapter 9

More Than Meets the Eye

In that August morning, 1991, at 7:15, Pam Reynolds, a 35-year-old woman from Atlanta, GA, was taken to the operating room. She was awake and (physically) conscious, but not for too long. Soon, the anesthetic given to her would send her into a deep sleep. Pam had suffered a basilar artery aneurysm (basilar is the most important artery in the back of the brain) and the only chance to avoid a rupture was to remove it. The surgical procedure would be extremely risky, and she could (physically) die on the operating table at the slightest mistake of the surgeon, or at the tiniest movement she might make.

The expert surgeon at that time was Dr. Robert Spetzler, Director of Barrow Neurological Institute in Phoenix, Arizona. He, together with a large number of other physicians, was going to lead the surgery to remove the aneurysm. For any chance of success, drastic measures had to be taken, beginning by draining the blood from the brain and blocking it from receiving more. In other words, Dr. Spetzler was going to flatline Pam's brain. To flatline her brain, blood circulation had to cease, and for it to cease the heart had to stop pumping. Dr. Spetzler had pioneered a technique known as hypodermic cardiac arrest, achieved by decreasing the body temperature to 60 degrees Fahrenheit. As you know, our normal body temperature is 98 degrees Fahrenheit; at this temperature all our organs function normally. But lower it to 60 degrees,[1] and the heart stops beating, breathing ceases, and with no blood going to the brain, brain waves flatten, a sign of no cerebral activity. As we have learned from conventional neuroscience, if the brain shuts down, it 'produces' no consciousness, thus 'brain-dependent' activities such as vision, hearing, feeling, thinking, memorization etc become absent.

Prior to the procedure when Pam was already under anesthesia, her hair was partially shaved; her eyes were lubricated to prevent drying and then taped shut. She could not see anything even if she was awake and conscious. In each ear a small molded speaker was inserted to monitor her auditory nerve cell, which also blocked sounds coming in. Therefore, in addition to being totally unconscious from anesthetic and later having a controlled cardiac arrest, Pam also had her eyes lubricated and shut with tape, and her hearing impaired by the insertion of the speakers.

Keeping these facts in mind, we can better appreciate what is going to happen to Pam once she gets flatlined. If human consciousness were produced by the brain as materialistic science postulates, in that state Pam could not see or hear anything, let alone move! Her legs and arms had been firmly tied down to prevent potential movement during the surgery, which could be fatal.

Yet nothing that had been done to her physical body prevented her from leaving it or from seeing and hearing, in minute details, what was happening in the operating room. And she went even farther—literally! Leaving the physical dimension, she rendezvoused with her departed loved ones waiting for her at the gates of heaven. This is one of—if not *the*—best documented cases of NDE in the history of NDE research, and a most extraordinary experience. Here is what Pam Reynolds told Dr. Michael Sabom, one of the pioneers in NDE research and a former skeptic:

The next thing I remember was the sound. It was a natural D (Pam was a singer). As I listened to the sound, I felt it was pulling me out of the top of my head. The further out of my body I got, the more clear the tone became. I had the impression it was like a road, a frequency that you go on... I remember seeing several things in the operating room when I was looking down. It was the most aware I think that I have ever been in my entire life... I was metaphorically sitting on Dr. Spetzler's shoulder. It wasn't like normal vision. It was brighter and more focused and clearer than normal vision... There was so much in the operating room that I didn't recognize and so many people. (Remember that her eyes were taped shut; she was under anesthetic and was physically unconscious.)

I thought the way they had my head shaved was very peculiar. I expected them to take all of the hair, but they didn't...

The saw thing (a Midas Rex bone saw) that I hated the sound of looked like an electric toothbrush and it had a dent in it (she had never seen one before), a groove at the top where the saw appeared to go into the handle, but it didn't... And the saw had interchangeable blades, too, but these blades were in what looked like a socket wrench case... I heard the saw crank up. I didn't see them use it on my head, but I think I heard it being used on something. It was humming at a relatively high pitch and then all of a sudden it went Brrrrrr! like that.

The saw was used to open Pam's skull, and while Dr. Spetzler was working on it, a female cardiac surgeon looked for the femoral artery and vein in Pam's right groin. Blood from these vessels was to feed the cardiopulmonary bypass machine, but the doctor found the vessels too small (and commented on it) so she prepared the vessels on the left groin instead, which were larger. Pam continued...

Someone said something about my veins and arteries being very small. I believe it was a female voice and that it was Dr. Murray, but I'm not sure. She was the cardiologist. I remember thinking that I should have told her about that... I remember the heart-lung machine (which was going to cool the blood). I didn't like the respirator... I remember a lot of tools and instruments that I didn't readily recognize.

Until this moment, about 10:50 a.m. (three hours and thirty-five minutes after being taken to the operating room), the cardiac arrest had not taken place. Pam's heart would be stopped a few minutes before the actual procedure began to remove the aneurism. The cardiac arrest and the absence of brain waves—flatline—occurred around 11:20 a.m. Five minutes later Dr. Spetzler began his spectacular and audacious surgical procedure. And that was when Pam Reynolds, under anesthetic, clinically dead, and with her arms and legs tied down, left the operating room for a taste of the other side of life.

There was a sensation like being pulled, but not against my will. I was going on my own accord because I wanted to go. I have different metaphors to try to explain this. It was like *The Wizard of Oz*—being taken up in a tornado vortex, only you're not spinning around like you've got vertigo. You're very focused and you have a place to go. The feeling was like going up in an elevator real fast. And there was a sensation, but it was not a bodily, physical sensation. It was like a tunnel but it was not a tunnel.

At some point very early in the tunnel vortex I became aware of my grandmother calling me. But I did not hear her call me with my ears... It was a clearer hearing than with my ears. I trust that sense more than I trust my own ears. The feeling was that she wanted me to come to her, so I continued with no fear down the shaft. It's a dark shaft I went through, and at the very end there was this very little pinpoint of light that kept getting bigger and bigger.

The light was incredibly bright, like sitting in the middle of a light bulb. It was so bright that I put my hands in front of my face fully expecting to see them and I couldn't. But I knew they were there. Not from a sense of touch. Again, it's terribly hard to explain, but I knew they were there...

I noticed that as I began to discern different figures in the light—and they were all covered with light, they were light, and had light permeating all around them—they began to form shapes I could recognize and understand. I could see that one of them was my grandmother. I don't know if that was reality or projection, but I would know my grandmother, the sound of her, anytime, anywhere.

Everyone I saw, looking back on it, fit perfectly into my understanding of what a person looked like at their best during their (earthly) lives.

I recognized a lot of people. My uncle Gene was there. So was my great-great-Aunt Maggie, who was really a cousin. On Papa's side of the family, my grandfather was there... They were specifically taking care of me, looking after me.

They wouldn't permit me to go further... It was communicated to me—that's the best way I know how to say it, because they didn't speak like I'm speaking—that if I went all the way into the light something would happen to me physically. They would be unable to put this me back into the body me, like I had gone too far and they couldn't reconnect. So they wouldn't let me go anywhere or do anything.

I wanted to go into the light, but I also wanted to come back. I had children to be reared. It was like watching a movie on fast-forward: You get a general idea, but the individual freeze-frames aren't slow enough to get detail.

In the operating room, Dr. Spetzler's amazing skills rapidly removed the aneurism, and the cardiopulmonary machine began to pump warm blood into Pam's arteries. Soon the heart and brain monitors began to register vital signs in Pam's still unconscious physical body. But she was not back yet!

Then they (the deceased relatives) were feeding me. They weren't doing this through my mouth, like with food, but they were nourishing me with something. The only way I know how to put it is something sparkly. Sparkles is the image that I get. I definitely recall the sensation of being nurtured and being fed and being made strong. I know it sounds funny, because obviously it wasn't a physical thing, but inside the experience I felt physically strong, ready for whatever.

Then suddenly, at 12:00 noon, something serious happened. The heart monitor, which had been silent up to that point, began to register disorganized cardiac activity indicating ventricular fibrillation, or a true cardiac arrest. Her body temperature was quickly raised, but it did not work. Two defibrillator paddles were quickly placed on Pam's chest, and 50 joules of electricity were shot down to her heart. To no avail. A hundred joules! Nothing. As the doctors began preparation to open Pam's chest to massage the heart itself, the cardiac rhythm began to normalize.

Pam was coming back.

My grandmother didn't take me back through the tunnel, or even send me back or ask me to go. She just looked up at me. I expected to go with her, but it was communicated to me that she just didn't think she would do that. My uncle said he would do it. He's the one who took me back through the end of the tunnel. Everything was fine. I did want to go.

But then I got to the end of it and saw the thing, my body, I didn't want to get into it... It looked terrible, like a train wreck. It looked like what it was: dead. I believe it was covered (indeed it was). It scared me and I didn't want to look at it.

It was communicated to me that it was like jumping into a swimming pool. No problem, just jump right into the swimming pool. I didn't want to, but I guess I was late or something because he (the uncle) pushed me. I felt a definite repelling and at the same time a pulling from the body. The body was pulling me and the tunnel was pushing... It was like diving into a pool of ice water... It hurt! [2]

If you, as a psychic nurse, were present at the moment of Pam's return to the operating room, you would have witnessed a spectacular scene. Pam, of course, had to resume her physical life, since her earthly journey had not been finished yet. "Everything was fine," she said. "I did want to go (back)." But time was ticking for the physical body. Upon seeing it in that condition, she refused to enter. And that was the time the heart monitor went berserk. The body was about to die. You would see that the pull of the silver cord was not strong enough to bring the spirit body back, since her unwillingness to return created an opposing force which pushed her away from the body, an other-worldly tug-of-war you were seeing for the first time. At 50 joules of shock to the heart, Pam was still resisting, but at 100 joules, and aided by her uncle's push, the cord pulled her in, and she was back. Again, you would see the spirit body coinciding with the physical, and notice at the same time the heart monitor going back to normal. At that point, you would join the medical team in their joyful celebration for having saved another life, physical life, that is, for the spirit never dies.

We are free spirits in more sense than one; this is our true nature. However, during the allotted time each one of us has been given to experience life on earth, the physical body keeps us in a temporary bondage. A bondage we routinely break for a few moments when the body is at rest, normally during sleep, and on episodes of out-of-body experiences when the body is healthy. We, as spirit that we are, "recover our freedom when the physical body becomes torpid. To leave the body, we take advantage of every moment of respite the body gives us. As soon as prostration of the vital forces occurs, we disengage from the body and the feebler the body, the easier it becomes to leave it."[3]

The physical body is feeblest when it dies, of course, and that is when we will find it the easiest to leave it. Next, is during NDE or a comatose period since there is nearly complete prostration of the vital forces, and the severer the case, the easier the exit. Though not all people who had a brush with death reported a NDE; as we have seen the statistics in Chapter 5, it does not necessarily mean that they did not have one. We all dream during sleep, but not everyone recalls her or his dreams. If you are reading this book it is because you have gone through a childhood phase and became an adult, but most likely you do not remember much—if at all—from your birth to about four or five years of age, for example. However, the fact that you do not have conscious memories of those years does not mean you did not exist during that period; otherwise, you would not be reading this book now. You did exist, even if you do not have conscious memories of that period.

Can't Tie Me Down

Maria's vital forces came into prostration during a cardiac arrest. From the moment she had been taken to her room, on the first floor of Harborview Medical Center in Seattle, Washington, four days earlier, she had been hooked up to cardiac monitor wires, from her chest to her calves. She was literally tied down to her bed and was unable to go anywhere, physically that is.

A middle-aged migrant worker, Maria had come to Seattle from the Yakima Valley to visit some friends when she suffered a massive heart attack. Her timely arrival to Harborview's coronary unit allowed doctors to bring her heartbeat and blood circulation under control. But on the morning of the fourth day, Maria's heart gave up again. And she flatlined. (Physically) unconscious, she was rapidly surrounded by emergency medical personnel who initiated resuscitation procedures. She received CPR, a tube was inserted down her trachea to bring oxygen to her lungs, and shock paddles placed on her chest to jump-start her heart. A couple of jolts later and Maria's heart was pumping again.

Our hearts can pump on and on, circulating blood to the tiniest vessel, bringing nutrients and oxygen to every cell that makes up the body's constitution, but if *we*, spirit that we are, are not present, the body is unconscious. And so was Maria's; she had vacated it and gone elsewhere. Confused as to what had happened to her, she had become extremely agitated upon her return to the body. So much so that the attending nurse was afraid she might have another heart attack.

When the nurse called Kimberly Sharp, Harborview's social worker, to calm Maria down, Maria told her what had happened. She had left her body and floated up to a corner near the ceiling; from there she watched what was happening down under, as medical personnel worked on reviving her body. Every detail she gave matched what had happened while the body was unconscious. Maria then ventured outside, floated past the emergency room entrance where ambulances brought patients in critical condition. What she said she had seen was verified by hospital staff. That was on the first floor. Out more and up, up past the second floor, window ledges in front of her, until she stopped. Something on the corner of a ledge of a room on the third floor caught her attention. Maria was hanging in mid air, eyeball to eyeball with a tennis shoe. While her body lay in bed in a room on the first floor, hooked up to monitor wires, unconscious and motionless, Maria, her true self, was free, all senses intact, unimpaired thinking capacity, perfect vision and ability to discern and memorize the tiniest details. In front of her a male tennis shoe, left foot, dark blue, worn out, scuffed where the little toe goes, and more, part of the lace was caught under the heel.

Intrigued by such minute details but not entirely credulous, contrary to the general naysayers, Kimberly Sharp gave Maria the benefit of doubt. Going first outside and walking around the entire building, the only part of third floor ledges visible from the ground was the bottom, a bit of the edges, but no shoe in sight, if there was any. Then she went inside the building, going from room to room on the third floor, pressing her face against the window of each room to catch a glimpse of the ledge corner from the inside. No shoe could be found. It was way past her quitting time and she was exhausted from a hard day's work. One more room and that was it. If no worn-out shoe on a ledge, the quest was over, and Maria's story would be just that, a story. But it was not just a story, it was a fact, and on the corner of the window ledge of the next room, there it was—the worn-out, dark blue left foot of a tennis shoe. A few minutes later, Maria, now back to the physical body but still hooked up to monitors, was holding the shoe Kimberly Sharp had brought to her, every detail matching her description.[4]

Near-death experiences (and OBEs) have proven repeatedly that we all have, living along with the physical body, an immaterial counterpart within which resides our true identity, the self we really are. It is the presence of this self, this identity in the physical body that gives it intelligence and maintains its conscious. When we are awake and active this identity is tightly united with the physical body, manifesting itself through it. Thus the impression we have is that the physical body is the totality of us humans. But given the proper condition, namely during a NDE or OBE, one can verify for oneself that she or he can, and will, continue living without a physical body. In this new condition, still possessing a body of a more subtle nature, no longer subject to the laws of gravity or bound to matter, one can roam freely both in physical and non-physical space. With all the senses intact, vision especially can be a boon. One can see long-gone dear relatives, like Pam Reynolds did, or find a shoe on a window ledge, as Maria did. Or use it for more practical down-to-earth purposes, such as...

Finding Lost Dentures

During the night shift, (wrote the attending nurse,) the ambulance crew brought in a forty-four-year-old cyanotic (purplish-blue skin discoloration), comatose man. About an hour earlier he had been found in a public park by passers-by, who had initiated heart massage. After admission to the coronary care unit, he received artificial respiration with a balloon and a mask as well as heart massage and defibrillation. When I wanted to change the respiration method, when I wanted to intubate the patient, the patient turned out to have dentures in his mouth. Before intubating him, I removed the upper set of dentures and put it on the crash cart. Meanwhile we continued extensive resuscitation. After approximately ninety minutes, the patient had sufficient heart rhythm and blood pressure, but he was still ventilated and intubated, and he remained comatose. In this state he was transferred to the intensive care unit for further respiration. After more than a week in a coma the patient returned to the coronary care unit, and I saw him when I was distributing the medication. As soon as he saw me he said, "Oh, yes, but you, you know where my dentures are." I was flabbergasted. Then he told me, "Yes, you were there when they brought me into the hospital, and you took the dentures out of my mouth and put them on that cart; it had all these bottles on it, and there was a sliding drawer underneath, and you put my teeth there."

I was all the more amazed because I remembered this happening when the man was in a deep coma and undergoing resuscitation. After further questioning, it turned out that the patient had seen himself lying in bed and that he had watched from above how nursing staff and doctors had been busy resuscitating him. He was also able to give an accurate and detailed description of the small room where he had been resuscitated and of the appearance of those present. While watching this scene, he had been terrified that we were going to stop resuscitating and that he would die. And it's true that we had been extremely negative about the patient's prognosis due to his very poor condition when admitted. The patient told me that he had been making desperate but unsuccessful attempts at letting us know that he was still alive and that we should continue resuscitating. He's deeply impressed by his experience and says he's no longer afraid of death.[5]

A Sad Sight

To be able to see someone's 'apparition' or spirit body when we are in the physical body we need psychic vision. The vibrational frequency of the spirit body is so subtle that physical eyes are unable to perceive it. And this is a blessing. We live immersed in the spirit world like fishes in the ocean; we would not live a sane life if we could see such a world while having to lead our physical life. With physical vision we can only see objects vibrating in the same frequency as our physical eyes, but once freed from matter we can see both worlds—the physical and the non-physical. But it may not always be a boon.

Hilda was traveling with her family in South Africa when they were involved in a serious auto accident. Hilda and her husband were ejected from the car:

> I was out of my body when I saw my children leaving the back seat and running to where my body was laying; I saw them trying to help me. I also saw my husband lying on the road, and I saw when he left his body and went towards a brilliant light in the distance. At that moment, I knew he had died.[6]

Remember your attempt to talk to your mother during your make-believe OBE? When out of our body, we can see things, and we can hear conversations going on, but unless people in the physical body have psychic hearing, they cannot hear us, no matter how dear they are to us or how hard we try.

Honey! Up Here!

I remember getting out of my body headfirst, floating over to the corner of the room. My wife was crying and I tried to tell her to look over here at me, that I was all right. But she wouldn't look at me. No one paid any attention. I moved past the two doctors and looked down at my body. The clothes had been burned from the fire and my face was a mess of peeling burnt skin.

The doctor said, "Is the machine charged to four hundred?" and then put two metal discs on my chest that were wired to the machine. I saw my body jump. It was then that I knew I had returned into my body. The pain felt like a mule had kicked me in the chest. This life was certainly worse than the other. I can still remember every detail.[7]

The people who experienced NDEs in the cases we have seen so far, had perfect physical vision, though their vision became impaired because of their physical unconsciousness. However, despite their lack of physical vision, when out of their body during clinical death, NDErs could still see, and in many cases what they saw was verified. Since these NDErs had healthy physical eyes, naysayers write off their purported visions as leftovers or residual visions of what they had seen prior to becoming physically unconscious.

But would it be possible that some visual mechanism unique to the non-physical body was at work during a NDE? If it were true that this new body had some kind of vision, could people born blind see during a NDE episode? Dr. Kenneth Ring, a psychology professor and NDE research pioneer and a founding member of the International Association for Near-Death Studies

(IANDS), posed a question to this nature. Boldly, he went out to test his hypothesis, and what he found was astounding.

Let us now marvel on Dr. Ring's findings.

Chapter 10

Through the Soul's Eyes
—NDE of the Blind

It was late night when Vicki Umipeg sang her last song in a Seattle nightclub. Unable to call a cab to take her home, the only other option was to ride in a Volkswagen van with a couple of patrons who had one too many drinks. Not long into the ride, a serious accident occurred, and Vicki was thrown out of the van. She suffered extensive injuries—skull fracture and concussion, damage to the neck and leg.

Vicki did not recall exactly how the accident happened. But remembered a scene that was extremely significant to her. When her body hit the hard and cold asphalt that night in early 1973, Vicki left her injured physical body and floated lightly up in the air. Looking down, she could *see* the crumpled van and the commotion around it.

Astonished, she realized that this new body was complete, but with a difference. Rather than being made of perishable matter, like the one laying unconsciously and nearly dead on the ground, the new one was indestructible, light, and flexible and made of "light", as she perceived it.

Soon the ambulance came and Vicki's body was taken to Harborview Medical Center's emergency room, the same hospital where Maria had seen the shoe on the window ledge.

I don't remember the trip to the hospital; next I noticed I was floating up on the ceiling, looking down at the man and woman working on the body. I knew it was me. I was pretty thin then. I was quite tall and thin at that point. And I recognized at first that it was a body, but I didn't even know that it was mine initially. Then I perceived that I was up on the ceiling, and I thought, 'Well, that's kind of weird. What am I doing up here?' I thought, 'Well, this must be me. Am I dead?' I just briefly saw this body, and... I knew that it was mine because I wasn't in mine. Then I was just away from it. It was that quick.

When we are in our spirit body matter is no barrier, ceilings and walls are just imaginary lines we can cross as though they were not even there. In an instant, Vicki was out of the building, looking down and having with her soul's eyes a panoramic view of the surroundings beneath. The freedom she felt was exhilarating. In this new body, there were no limitations, no impairment, and no force binding it to the ground. Only wholeness, lightness, and... music. But not that kind of music you hear with ears; this was the kind you feel with your soul. To Vicki it was even more than this. It was a bridge which would take her to the other side of life. Through a dark tunnel she went, moving fast toward a light, and the music, which before was marvelous, was now sublimely so. Rolling out of the tunnel, Vicki found herself lying on a grass field. Glancing around, something her physical eyes could never do, she saw trees and flowers and a large number of people. And light, light that you would not just see but feel as well. Everywhere there was light.

What we think of death, what we term the loss of a loved one, is but a temporary separation of a soul who has finished its earthly work from those lagging behind in the physical plane. The people we meet on this earth, those with whom we share our joys and sorrows, our pains and pleasures, such as our children, our relatives, and close friends, are evolutionary mates we have been around from time immemorial. And we will reunite!

Vicki saw, out of the crowd, a welcoming committee she had known before and were dear to her, five souls in all. Debby and Diane were Vicki's blind schoolmates who had (physically) died years before. Debby when she was eleven and Diane when she was six. Both had been severely impaired intellectually, and blind as well. But not anymore. Now they were healthy, bright and beautiful, and no longer children, but in their prime. Mr. and Mrs. Zilk, who had been Vicki's caretakers and now inhabitants of the spiritual side of life, still together as a couple, still sharing their love and care for each other, were also present to greet her. The fifth soul was a special one; she had been in the spirit side of life for just two years. She had practically raised Vicki, but Vicki, having no physical sight, had never seen her face in the twenty years they had spent together on the physical plane. But now, as her dear Grandma walked over to give her a warm and loving hug, now free from the limitations of the physical body lying unconscious in Harborview Medical Center, Vicki, for the first time, could see her dear Grandmother.

Vicki felt a presence by her side, a radiant being she had met years before when she had had her first NDE as a child. To her, this presence was Jesus, and there was no other place in the universe she wanted to be more. She wanted to be there, by his side, healthy and free as she now was. And Vicki was about to find out that Jesus also has a sense of humor.

"Isn't it wonderful?" He said. "Everything is beautiful here, everything fits together. And you'll find that."

She could not agree more after all she had seen and felt in that place, but then came the spoiler. "But you cannot stay here now. It's not your time to be here yet and you have to go back."

Vicky protested, "No, I want to stay with you!"

"I know," said Jesus. "And you will be back when your time comes, but now you have to return..."

And here it is again, coming from the mind of the Master himself the reason why Vicki needed to come back. Her earthly life had been short, just twenty-two years when she had the accident.

"... You have to return to learn and teach more about loving and forgiving."

Vicki understood the message, but still wanted to stay. When Jesus told her she would marry and have children, something she dearly wanted, she agreed. Before returning, she had a panoramic view of her twenty-two years of earthly life, from the day of her birth to the moment of the accident. As images came into view, Jesus would make loving comments, telling her the significance of every action and the consequences thereof.

"You have to leave now," were the last words she heard from Him. Then like a roller coaster going backwards, she was drawn back to her body. Feeling heavy and full of pain, she found herself back to physical life, her eyesight blackened by the deficiencies of her visual organs. Vicki will see no more until the day she leaves her body again. Later on, Vicky married and had three children, as Jesus had told her she would.[1]

When we, indestructible spirit that we are, immerse ourselves in physical matter to experience life on earth, we become subject to the conditions and limitations of the material body. Though the physical body is not *us*, we live in extremely close association with it and are highly dependent on it to interact with physical life. So close are we that for most of our life, if not our entire earthly existence, we identify ourselves with the body we carry around, not with the spirit that makes it live. Our body may be missing a limb or all limbs, but *we*, the spirit animating it, are intact, for we are not the body. Our body may have damaged eardrums, but once out of it, we, in our spirit body, will hear. Free from matter, we will communicate, even if the physical body restricts it when we are immersed in it. The eyes of the body may be blind, but the eyes of the soul are wide open. And once free, we will see—each one of us—that the light of joy and peace shines for all.

Sweet Sounds of Heaven

Brad Barrows was not feeling well that week, and his condition worsened that night. He had trouble breathing, felt tired, had been coughing, and began to run a fever. His condition was making him very weak. At just eight years of age, blind, living with a roommate at the Boston Center for Blind Children, Brad was scared. He thought he was dying. In the morning, about 6:30 or 7:00, his breathing began to slow down, then ceased, and his heart stopped beating.

As breathing and heartbeat slowed down, Brad's physical body began to loosen the ties binding the spirit counterpart to it. He began to move out and float towards the ceiling with the lightness of a soap bubble. He went through the ceiling, and found himself out in the open sky of that cold winter morning. But in that new body, he felt no cold. In fact, he may not have even been concerned about temperature; there was something else drawing his full attention. Something else he had never experienced before in his life. Blind from birth in his physical body, he could now see for the first time through the soul's eyes.

Just before crossing the ceiling, he saw his scared blind roommate getting up and groping his way out for help; then his own motionless body lying in bed drew his attention. And he would see more. Out of the building and floating freely, with all his senses intact, he could see the cloudy and dark sky up above, and down below snow everywhere, except for the slushy streets which had been plowed. He saw snowbanks lining the deserted streets, and a bus driving by. Seeing for the first time the playground and the nearby hill where he played with other children delighted him.

Then came the time to go beyond, and Brad was pulled into a tunnel. But unlike Callahan Tunnel beneath Boston Harbor which connects one physical part of the city to another, NDE tunnels are bridges between dimensions—the physical and non-physical. So rather than landing at Logan International Airport or Route 1A if it were Callahan Tunnel, Brad landed on an "immense field stretching for what seemed like miles. I knew that somehow I could sense and literally see everything that was around me," he said as an adult.[2]

Surrounded by huge palm trees spread through a lush field of radiant tall grass, Brad found himself walking on a path. The feeling was ineffable, the beauty astounding. He was ecstatic, certain he had returned home, wherever this home was.

When I noticed that I was walking up this field, it seemed as if I was exhilarated and so unbelievably renewed... that I... didn't want to leave. I wanted to stay forever where I was. The only way I could describe it adequately would be that it was a feeling that I had as if I were home, and I didn't want to leave... It was so unbelievably peaceful that there is no way I could describe the peace and the tranquility and the calmness... [The] weather was absolutely perfect in terms of temperature and humidity. It was so fresh, so unbelievably fresh...

The other thing I noticed was that I knew there was something beyond the senses that I'd never had on earth that told me there was tremendous light up there. It seemed to come from every direction... It was all around and everywhere that I happened to be looking... I recall that vividly. It seemed to be all-encompassing. It seemed like everything, even the grass I had been stepping on and the leaves on the palm trees, were soaked in that light... Yet I wondered how I could know that because I had never seen (with physical eyes) before that point...

Brad's physical body, now lying unconscious in his bedroom in the school dorm, was visually impaired, but the hearing was perfect. But even if physical hearing were also impaired, it would not prevent Brad, now in his perfect spirit body, to hear what he heard.

... [M]any, many thousands of human voices... that seemed to be singing in a language I had never understood or maybe many, many languages. The music I had heard was nothing like anything I have ever experienced on earth... The rhythms were extremely thrilling and very gentle, almost like you hear in New Age music.

The journey was magical, the sounds divine. Brad wanted to add his own voice to the music, for the feeling he had was that all these voices were singing their praise to a Being they were about to meet—the Creator himself.

"And I wanted to see this being. I wanted to be with him forever," Brad recalled.

Ahead at a distance, a massive and marvelous glittering stone structure appearing to be made of light drew his attention. The light was so intense that for a moment Brad feared it might burn him, but forward he went. Upon entering the structure, he realized he was walking inside a huge tube, and the music was now more vivid, more heavenly-like. He felt as though getting closer to the source. And that's exactly where he wanted to go, to the source. In awe of the music, he kept advancing, but unbeknownst to him, there was a point he could not cross. It was not his time to cross it yet. A large and firm arm, from a Being whose presence made him comfortable and loved, stopped him from going forward. No words were exchanged, but Brad felt he'd have to return, even though he wanted to stay.

The Being gave Brad a gentle push backward, and he began his return trip. He crossed the radiant field of tall grass and palm trees, entered the tunnel again. Back to the physical plane, he saw the school building, crossing the walls went to his room, and entered his body. Brad gasped for air and felt the heaviness of his material body; opening his eyes he stared at the familiar darkness of his impaired vision.

When Jesus and his disciples passed a man blind from birth, they asked: "Master, who sinned that this man was born blind, himself or his parents?" And Jesus answered: "Neither has sinned, but that the works of God should be manifest in him."[3]

The physical body we now possess, either perfect or imperfect, is neither a reward for our being good nor a punishment for our being bad. It is exactly what we need in order to learn the lessons we came here to learn, or to teach. By doing the best we can with the body and resources we have, the works of God are manifested in us. Physical impairments are temporary inconveniences which help us progress spiritually. They can teach us and others love, patience, faith, creativity, perseverance, compassion, abnegation—virtues that enrich the soul and put us ever so closer to the divine realms we will one day reach.

We learn from Vicki and Brad that blindness is an inconvenience imposed by the physical body, existing during earthly life, which, once finished, vision will be fully restored. And Debbie, another NDEr born blind, corroborates that blindness is an impairment of the body not of the soul.

Home, Sweet Home

Debbie had two NDEs, the first one when she was 25 years old. She had suffered serious burn injuries for which she had been hospitalized for over two months. Brushing her teeth one morning as she convalesced at home, she lost (physical) consciousness. Emerging free from the limitations of her body, she was able to pierce through the tenuous veil that separates the physical and spiritual realities, which we all live immersed in, even if we are not aware of it.

Contrary to the NDEs of Vicki and Brad, who experienced the spiritual realm independently of the physical, Debbie straddled realities. Out of her body, she could perceive both the physical and non-physical realms at the same time. As it is in the case of *all* NDEs (and OBEs), without one single exception, Debbie's locus of consciousness was in the spirit body, while the physical lay motionless and unconscious on the floor. Now with her vision fully restored and expanded, what she saw astounded her.

First was the light. Light of indescribable colors enveloped her. At the same time she could see the physical environment— her unconscious body lying on the floor and her mother bent over checking on it. This was the very first time ever Debbie had seen her mother and her own body.

From the other side of life, a Being approached Debbie, comforting her, helping her cross a bridge. A (physically) deceased grandmother, young looking now, whom she had never seen or met, introduced herself. Proving that the ties of love never break and death never do us part, the grandmother showed Debbie friends and ancestors belonging to the huge spiritual family she had always been a part of.

Then a pleasantly unexpected surprise as she heard a familiar voice calling her name.

"Hi, Debbie!"

The recognition was instantaneous, though this was the very first time ever Debbie had *seen* her childhood friend.

"Oh, Darlene!"

Darlene, now thin and healthy, had suffered from kidney and thyroid problems, which caused the death of her body. So happy was Debbie in the spirit world that she, like the great majority of NDErs, did not want to return. She pleaded with the Being to let her stay. But she could not. As she kept insisting to stay, the Being showed her earthly future, as he had done to Vicki. Debbie was shown the person she was going to marry, and the beautiful girl they would have. She returned to complete her earthly life, married to the man she was shown, and did have a baby girl. Though blind since birth, in both her NDEs, Debbie had perfect vision.[4]

Dr. Kenneth Ring, with the help of several organizations for the blind, identified twenty-one visually impaired persons who had undergone a near-death experience. Vicki Umipeg and Brad Barrows, whose experiences we just saw, were born blind. Debbie was born with vision, but, being premature, she was put in an incubator and given too much oxygen, which caused the loss of her sight. The remaining NDErs had lost their vision in childhood; others had extremely limited sight, such as the ability to distinguish light and dark only. Out of these twenty-one NDErs, fifteen reported having seen images; three could not tell whether they had normal vision while out of their body, only three said they could not see anything.[5]

We have seen here only three of the fifteen cases who reported vision during their NDE—Vicki, Brad, and Debbie. And what did the other twelve who had vision during their NDE see while out of their body? Basically the same the other three reported. Indeed, similar to what millions of NDErs around the world have reported! First the feeling of leaving the body; then seeing the lifeless physical body; leaving the place where the physical body lies; landing in a spiritual realm; seeing discarnate relatives and friends; a radiant light; meeting a Being of Light; and so on.

The great American psychologist and philosopher of the late 1800s, Harvard Professor William James, on investigating human immortality quipped that to prove that not all crows are black all we need to find is one white crow. "... [I]n science 'one' white crow destroys your theory that 'all crows are black'."[6] To prove that the spirit body has perfect vision and that the visually impaired—indeed, all of us—will continue living and seeing after we leave the physical body, Dr. Kenneth Ring found fifteen white crows—a number far greater than one!

A Reason for Being

Our existence has a purpose, even if many a time it seems otherwise. Two thousand years ago, Jesus told us what the purpose was: "Be perfect, as our Father who is in heaven is perfect."[7] Not an easy task, to say the least. Knowing that, our

Father gave us eternity, plenty of time to catch up. However, it is expected from us that in every phase of our eternal existence we take a step ahead, move forward, even if just a tad at a time. However, quite often we come to a halt. We get too engrossed in doing things we should avoid, rather than doing things that help us grow. So we stagnate. Or worse still as we may even engage in hurtful behavior, causing pain not only to ourselves, but also to those we share our life with and who hold us dear. But forward we must move. It is a divine law creation must obey. And when we are too far off the road of progress, life finds a way to awake us from our slumber.

If you have or have had teenage children, you would know how hard it is sometimes to wake them in the morning to go to school. We might even have to pull the sheet from under them, or drag them out of bed, or shake them hard until they show a sign of life. We might lose our temper in the process and scream and vow to ground them if they are late for school or get bad grades. We do all this because we love them, not because we do not. If we did not we would not go through all this trouble. For loving us so much, our heavenly Father also has His ways of shaking us awake when we are oversleeping and running behind in the great school of life that earth is. NDE is a case in point, a powerful jolt that can change a life around.

So far, the NDEs we have seen are filled with radiant light and ineffable beauty, so much so that NDErs, even though they might have been scared of dying prior to the experience, once they catch a glimpse of the afterlife awaiting for them, they want to stay. But not all NDEs are as glorious. To those running behind or who stray too far away from the right track, the message is bleak. As bad as life on earth might have been for them, it becomes paradise in comparison to where they end up after crossing to the other side. Staying there does not even cross their minds; they want to come back—and fast!

We are in this life to learn, and learn we will. Learning here comes in two basic ways, easy and hard. Since we have already attained a level of consciousness that tells us that suffering is not a good thing, we should all strive to learn the easy way, unless we have a penchant for masochism. Even though we have attained a level of consciousness that tells us there is an easy way to learn things, apparently not everybody is aware of it; some still chose the hard and painful road. And they can be our teachers. Let us now see what those who have learned the hard way can teach us so that we do not make the same mistake.

Chapter 11

A Bitter Taste of Nothingness

Jay loved the pleasures of the senses, and there could not be a better place to live to gratify his urges than the Sin City, as Las Vegas is nicknamed. Gambling and drugs were his favorite pastimes. A successful young man, money posed no problem. His shake-awake moment came one night at a party doing drugs.

I died. I left my body and went into an outer darkness and it was eternity. It was a void, incredibly painful. It felt like forever. I know what the meaning of hell is, because it was hell. I was in hell! It was the absence of everything: the absence of love and emotions, just an absolute emptiness. I will never forget the pain. It wasn't physical at all. That's what was so terrifying. It was emotional, psychological, and spiritual pain. My spirit had descended into this place. I was convinced that I was never coming back.

I saw my life somewhere along the way. It was very brief. I felt the whole thing was a judgment. I saw it as a warning. I cried up to God and it was by the power of God and the mercy of God that I was permitted to come back. It was just so intense!

I think God is in control of everything that happens. I think it was a warning from God saying: "You are going to wind up here," meaning if I do anything to myself. No matter how bad it is here, it cannot compare to there. Death is a lot worse than life if you don't help God.

I think what happened was a blessing in disguise. I've stopped drugs, moved back to Florida, and now I'm in Bible College. I used to have a casual attitude about death, but now I actually fear it more. Life on earth is very brief, but eternity is forever. So, yes it was a warning. I was permitted another chance to change my behavior on earth. I've taken the fear of death and given it to the scriptures, but everyone should know that there is no finality with death.[1]

In the beginning of the book, I said that during one of my OBEs I jumped on my left leg to find out if my bad knee hurt, and I did not feel any pain. NDErs who have been in pain prior to leaving the physical body report the pain gone once they are in the spirit body. We just read Jay telling us about the pain he went through, but it was not physical. Jay did not report going to the traditional hellfire of fundamentalist religions, but even if he had, he would not have felt any physical pain either. And here is why. Being imperishable, the spirit body does not have and does not require a nervous system in its anatomy as the physical body does. Therefore, nociceptors or nerve endings that tell us through physical pain whether we have been hurt and help us protect against potentially damaging stimuli, such as fire, are not present in the spirit body. Pain response mechanism is a biological function of the physical body that helps us preserve it and keep it running in good condition while we experience earthly life. And since the spirit body is not physical, no physical pain will ever be felt, of course. However, worse than any physical pain is the pain of a guilty and remorseful consciousness. There is no medication to relieve such a discomfort other than redemption for the wrongdoings that caused it. And if not cured it will haunt us, both in this life and in the next. For when we die, we discard the physical body only; all the memories of what we have been and all that we have done come with us, to sweeten or to sour our future existence, according to how we lived while on earth. We carry ourselves around wherever we go, be it in this life or in the next. There is no escape from this reality.

Change Your Life or...

I had severe abdominal pains from an inflammatory condition in the pancreas. They were giving me medicine for my blood pressure which was falling and my consciousness was slipping. I remember them working on me. I was going through a long tunnel and I was wondering why my feet weren't touching the sides. I seemed to be floating and going very fast. It seemed to be underground. It may have been a cave, but the awfullest, eerie sounds were going on. There was an odor of decay like a cancer patient would have. Everything now seemed to be in slow motion. I cannot recall all of the things I saw, but some of the workers were only half human, mocking and talking to each other in a language I didn't understand. When you ask me if I saw anybody I knew or if I met a Being of Light, I didn't. But there was a large person in radiant white clothes that appeared when I called, "Jesus, save me!" He looked at me and I felt the message, 'Live differently!' I don't remember leaving there or how I got back. There are many other things that may have happened that I don't remember. Maybe I'm afraid to remember![2]

No hell is forever, unless we stay forever on the road that leads to it. In our eternal existence, we are blessed with the freedom of doing with our life whatever we want to do. But we also live in a universe governed by inexorable physical and divine laws, cause and effect being an inescapable one. It is this law that determines the nature of our life (effect)—either on earth or in the beyond—dictated by the quality of our thoughts, emotions, and actions (cause). "Be not deceived," wrote Paul to the Galatians, "God is not mocked: for whatsoever a man sows, that shall he also reap."[3]

Indeed, we cannot mock God, and our derailments from His laws will cost us dearly. And no one can be blamed but us; we must own the consequences of the decisions we have made as to how we lead our life. In the current stage of our evolution, where most of us identify ourselves with the physical body we are wearing rather than the spiritual beings we really are, we make many mistakes. Depending on the severity of our mistakes, the consequences they will bring may throw us in the depths of hell even if we are still in physical life. But either in this life or in the next, hell only lasts as long as we persist doing the actions that keep it on fire. Once we change course, hell vanishes, for hell is neither a creation of the devil nor of God, but of our own. Regardless how deeply immersed we are in it at any time in our life, God is always on our side, hands stretched, ready to pull us out of our agonizing darkness and give us another chance.

Escaping from Hell

Dennis, a recovering alcoholic, had his shake-awake moment at thirty-five during a NDE as a consequence of a ruptured appendix.

I was going in and out of coma. At one point I was in so much pain from surgery, staples, drains, and tubes that it was hard to keep fighting. I couldn't communicate. I was lying in bed and all of a sudden I was removed from myself. I was up on the ceiling looking down on this thin, frail body, and for the first time I realized how sick I was. Then the room started getting darker and darker. It was like a void of life. It was the absence of light.

I felt bound in the darkness, like a weight was holding me down. It was what I grew up to know as hell. Right before me the total darkness. I reviewed my life. For the most part it was things that I was disappointed in myself about. It was like a fast-forward of scenes. I got the sense that it wasn't the particular scenes that were important, but what was important was that I felt it was just so much of a waste. Like, wow, there's nothing there! Then I saw these black fragments that started to move. I realized they were silhouettes, shadows of people, and I could hear chains being pulled. I heard moans and I got terrified.

I thought they were my ancestors coming for me, and I didn't want to go. In the middle of all this was a little flicker of light, like a small birthday candle light. Something told me not to look at the darkness, but to just keep looking at the light. And I said: "God, I'm ready to go if you want me, but I've led such a useless life I'd like another chance to put it right," and just at that point a sword came up through the candle, through the flicker of light, and the whole room lit up. I dropped back into my body and could hear the doctors and nurses saying: "He's alive!"

I fell away from the Church at about twelve or thirteen. I have found my faith again now through Alcoholics Anonymous. Since my death experience I've returned to Church... The feeling I got (from the NDE) was redemption. Hell was the place I was bound for, but not a place that I have to go now. I had a choice. I think that was the key to it. It was when I asked God what I did that I made the choice, and the choice is there for all of us, all the time. I feel that I'm an emissary of sorts. When I think someone has tried walking toward the light but now they're blocked, I'll tell them my story. I know I wasn't supposed to hoard this experience to myself. It was for other people too.[4]

Negative NDEs

Experiences such as these we have just seen are called *negative*, *distressing*, or *less-than-positive* NDEs; perhaps *distressing* is the best qualifier. While these experiences lack the radiance and glory of most NDEs, they do cause an extremely positive effect on the NDEr. In the cases above, all three NDErs changed their lives for the better. And the same is true in other cases of distressing NDEs that have been reported. This is just one of the strange ways God employs to wake us from our spiritual torpor.

My Shake-Awake Turn

To get back on the spiritual path I had strayed from, I had to suffer financial ruin at age forty-six, with a wife and a five-year-old daughter to support, $200 I had left, and a Bible on which to cry my misery, a misery of my own creation. Neither God nor the devil was punishing me, for God is only love and compassion, and the devil a convenient fiction we can use to pass on responsibilities that are ours. The consequences of my own mistakes were punishing me; I was simply reaping what I had sown. I had no one to blame but me.

Being the only book in my possession, I sought comfort and help in the Bible. I opened it to the message I needed. I sobbed as I read and understood it. And the message told me that I could change my whole life, but I had to take action and do things, move forward. Nothing is still in the universe. The very millions of atoms that compose the pages of the book you are holding — and of your entire body — are moving, even if you do not see or feel them. You can feel the heat as you pay attention to the tips of your fingers holding the page. This is movement, this is action, this is life.

"Ask, and it shall be given you; seek, and ye shall find; knock, and it shall be opened unto you: For every one that asketh receiveth; and he that seeketh findeth; and to him that knocketh it shall be opened."[5] What a powerful call to action! These were the very words I read, transcribed here from the very copy of the Bible I read them from, a copy I hold dearly to this day. If you still have doubts that God works in strange ways, I had 'borrowed' this Bible from a hotel I had stayed at several years before, but had barely opened it until that day. The day I needed it the most, and read the words that gave my life a new direction.

When we travel in the right direction, when we act to improve our lot, when we open our heart and soul to life, life pours its blessings on us. And we, in turn, can help better the lot of those around us and who depend on us. That is how each one of us fulfills, even if just a tiny bit this time around, our part in the works of creation, which has been, even if most of us do not know, assigned to us by our loving Creator. Life is action, life is movement, life is a circle...

And it moves us all
Through despair and hope
Through faith and love
Till we find our place
On the path unwinding
In the Circle of Life.[6]

However, sometimes despair is greater than hope, and we believe that if we end this life, we solve all our problems. In my own despair, many a time I thought of that as an option. But knowing that life never ends, that I would be adding insult to my misery, I chose to act. Regardless of how deep our wounds are and how much we are hurting, we will be healed. And we will re-emerge stronger. All we need is faith, patience, and perseverance. Time is on our side, and we are protected; we never walk alone even if we do not see anybody around. Physical life is an educational process, a training ground that at times exhausts our energy, our faith, our patience, and our hopes. But we must not yield. We are growing; we are becoming better. *Grin and bear it* must be our daily battle cry until we cross the dark valley lying before us. We are in this life to heal others and ourselves; we are not here to hurt, neither us nor anyone else, for physical life is a precious gift that nobody has the right to destroy.

And those who tried to destroy it sorely regretted; we can learn from them and avoid walking the same path.

Chapter 12

Suicide, a Mistaken Choice

Talking on the phone with my teenage daughter the other day, she told me her friend Randy, a teenager like her, was missing. "He took off on his bike carrying a gun," she said. "He left a note to his mom saying that humankind was filled with scumbags and the world was about to end and he was not going to wait around for it." He was depressed. Three days later his body was found on the roof of a local public school, shot to death. A couple of years ago, another friend of hers, also a teenager, hung himself because of family problems. Many bullying victims are also making this mistaken choice out of despair.

According to the US Centers for Disease Control and Prevention, in 2010 suicide was the tenth leading cause of death for all ages. In the US alone more than 38,000 people took their own lives that year, over 100 suicides every day.[1] Killing our body will not extinguish our life nor will it solve our problems. As we will see below, NDErs who thought they would find a shortcut to their problems by cutting short their lives bitterly regretted it. It behooves us to learn from their mistakes rather than our own. We can seek help to deal with and to solve our temporary problems. It is possible. We can solve them. With faith, patience, and guidance we will be healed.

Hanging in There — Literally!

At age 48, the woodworker wanted to take a nice vacation with his wife, for which he had been saving for years. Shortly before his vacation, he was arrested for drunk driving. His license was suspended and he was heavily fined, losing all the money he had saved for his dreamed vacation. Despondent over his troubles, he tried a shortcut to end his misery.

From the roof of the utility shed in my backyard I jumped to the ground. Luckily for me I had forgotten the broken lawn chair that lay near the shed. My feet hit the chair and broke my fall, or my neck would have been broken. I hung in the rope and strangled. I was outside my physical body. I saw my body hanging in the rope; it looked awful. I was terrified; I could see and hear, but it was different—hard to explain. Demons were all around me. I could hear them but couldn't see them. They chattered like blackbirds. It was as if they knew they had me, and had all eternity to drag me down into hell, to torment me. It would have been the worst kind of hell, trapped hopelessly between two worlds, wandering lost and confused for all eternity.

I had to get back into my body. Oh my God, I needed help. I ran to the house, went in through the door without opening it, cried out to my wife but she couldn't hear me, so I went into her body. I could see and hear with her eyes and ears. Then I made contact, heard her say, "Oh, my God."

She grabbed a knife and ran out to where I was hanging and got up on an old chair and cut me down. She could find no pulse; she was a nurse. When the emergency squad got to me my heart had stopped; my breath too was gone.[2]

God Doesn't Give Up on Us

Sometimes our spiritual slumber becomes a heavy sleep, and it is really hard to shake us awake. But God does not give up on us, and He will keep trying until we get up and get moving. Shandra was from a rich family. A successful makeup artist for TV and movies, she lived a glamorous life in the fast lane. From the outside, the big mansion she lived in caused envy to those not used to a rich life, but for her, who was inside, life was miserable. She had an abusive father, who used to hit her violently. To escape from pain she went into drugs, and from drugs to hell— four times—until she got the message.

I swallowed a bottle of 100 Quaaludes in California and remember just fading and hearing people call my family to tell them I was dead. I'm on this steel table in a dark room at USC Medical Center in LA. I just remember looking down from above at this humongous black nurse. She was basically like yelling at my body saying: "You stupid girl!" I know I actually saw my family, even though I was in California and they were in New York. So I traveled that far without my (physical) body.

I didn't want to die, but I didn't not want to die. I was in some holding place that was dark, with just a ray of light. There were shadowy figures, and I heard music, definitely angelic music, that had a semi-Christian tinge to it. The entities were telling me: "You have to go back." The message was: 'You have a purpose and lessons to learn in this lifetime.' I was getting spoken to and coached on coming back. I was told I had to find answers out for myself. See, I wasn't given information. I wasn't open to it because there was so much pain in me. I thought I wanted to die, or at least I didn't want to be in pain, and I didn't know how not to be. All four times I was in that same holding place.

I was brought up in a Jewish home and was taught that when you die you just go to sleep forever, which to me was good comfort, because I didn't want to have to deal with anything. But now I know that if you commit suicide, you don't just go to sleep, but you have to do it again. You have to learn your lessons.

That sliver of light was perfect with the darkness, because I was saying to me: 'You can get out of here.' In other words, just do it! Do it! To me, hell is separation from God and we do that to ourselves. I think if you believe in hell, then you'll be in it. Even though it was mostly dark, I felt safe where I was, but the message was to get out because you don't belong here. So I got exactly what I needed and I think that's how it works.

After the fourth one I finally got the message and went into a drug rehab program in Florida. It was the stepping stone for me to do some housecleaning. I was twenty-four, knew I had to get off drugs, and when I did get clean I spent seven years in Florida dedicating my life to working with teenagers on drugs and their families. The best thing of all was I married the man who was program director... Back then I just wasn't getting it. I wasn't understanding... that the answer to everything is love. And I don't need another NDE.[3]

Ask and You Shall Receive

We just heard Shandra saying that she thinks hell is a separation from God. I was once visiting a terminally ill patient in his final weeks of physical life. Prior to his diagnosis, he was not religious. He was an old man, in his late seventies, and knew he was dying. In that visit I asked him: "How do you spend your days now that you have no place to go?" The answer was immediate: "I pray all day. That's what I do now." NDE literature is rife with cases of atheists and agnostics who became spiritual (not necessarily religious) after their transforming experience. When everything is going smoothly in our lives, we tend to forget about God, priding ourselves on our self-sufficiency. But when we are in trouble and alone, that's who we clamor to for help, God. And God, with all His love and knowing what is best for us, gives if we ask. Rochelle was a proud agnostic, until the day she felt the bitter taste of darkness, after which she renewed her faith and redirected her life.

I tried suicide twice. The first time was an overdose and I was in the hospital for a month, but I didn't have an experience. Then I did it again. This time I turned the gas on. Up north they have those old radiators. Well, I was in a state of depression and I couldn't stop crying. I couldn't sleep to get away from it. At the time I wasn't a believer. I didn't believe there was anything after you died. I was agnostic. I didn't believe there was a devil or a heaven or hell. So I thought the only way to get rid of this pain was to end it all. I sealed up the windows and the door, turned on the gas, and lay down on the bed and went right off to sleep.

Well, all of a sudden I was in this dark place, blackness, total blackness. No light, just a black void. I knew in my mind I was dead, but I took the pain with me. All the pain I was suffering I took with me. So I thought: 'Oh, my goodness, I'm going to have to go through this for an eternity!' Then something touched me on the shoulder, and I looked around and here's this big gorilla, or this ape. Now, for some reason, I associated this ape with Satan. I knew I had died and was in hell and would have to suffer like this for eternity, with this heartache I had, and this pain. I screamed from the pits of my soul. I screamed out for God and I screamed and kept screaming. Finally, He pulled me up and BOOM, I woke up! It was three or four hours later, there was gas all over this three-story house, but I wasn't even nauseated. It was like God was saying: "Look, I've had enough of this foolishness. There is something after this life," and He showed it to me and pulled me out of it.

I would like people who are in the position I was in, depressed, to know that if they think they're going to escape it by dying, I would like to tell them: no you will not! If you die you'll still have to live in that pain, because you don't really die, so it doesn't do anything. You cannot escape it, so don't try to kill yourself. You're going to have to work your way through this and you CAN work your way through it with help. There is help out there.[4]

Here or There, We Are What We Are

I was born in a Third World country. Let me expand on that. I was born on a farm, in a one-room hut, behind a cemetery, with no electricity, no running water, no indoor bathroom, and (I feel sorry for my mother) no diapers, in the interior of a Third World country. I lived on a farm until I was eight years old. There were small towns and cities nearby, which were more advanced than the precarious farm I lived on. I learned all about farm life as the first eight years of my earthly life allowed me, but I knew nothing about city life. I had never lived in one before. When I moved to one of those cities, the knowledge I brought with me was what I had learned on the farm. Life in the city was different. Accent was different. People lived closer to each other. They had habits that were new to me. There were more social activities. Some houses even had a box in their living room with tiny people inside, so when I saw Barnabas Collins seeing a TV set for the first time, I knew the feeling. When I moved from the farm to the city only one thing changed in my life—the location where I was living. My name remained the same; my likes and dislikes remained the same; my gender remained the same; the knowledge I had acquired up to that point in my life did not increase just because I was transported from one place to another. Or because city life was more advanced than farm life, I became automatically more advanced just for having moved to a more advanced place. Of course, I did acquire new habits and new knowledge, but as time went by, not immediately.

For the next twenty years I lived in Brazil, six years in that city and another fourteen in the largest city of the country. Throughout those years I learned from living, from working, and from academic studies. I gained knowledge, acquired experience in several areas, developed a personality, a character, a uniqueness that sets me apart from others. And I obviously learned the official language of the country, Portuguese.

In 1982 I moved to America, a country far more advanced than the one I was coming from. Starting on the plane, the airline crew communicated with me in English, which I struggled to understand. Coming out of the plane upon arrival, I heard

English all around, and being in Miami, Spanish too. The immigration officer spoke to me in English, and I struggled to understand and reply as well. I was in another country, indeed in another continent in another hemisphere, but nothing in me had changed. The fact that my new home country was far more advanced than my old one, per se, did not change me a bit as I arrived. The very same *me* that had left Brazil eight hours before arrived in Miami. The same set of knowledge, the same amount of acquired experience, the same personality, and character, and uniqueness that I had in me prior to my arrival, landed in Miami. The only thing that had changed in that wonderful adventure was the location where I was present. But I was still the same. Of course I am not the same as thirty years ago. I grew in many aspects I did not have the chance to while in my country. I learned both languages spoken in Miami. I pursued academic studies. I raised children. I opened business. I wrote books. And I am still growing and developing, just like you and everyone else who had the courage to incarnate on this amazing planet. My progress came in time, as consequence of my interests and efforts, not just because I arrived in America.

I have no plans to move out of Miami in what remains of my lot in this physical life. The spiritual realms will be my next destination. And when that time comes, there will be two changes, instead of one. First it is the body I will be manifesting in, a lighter and subtler one, and second the location in which I will be functioning, a non-physical dimension compatible with my level of development. Nothing more. The wisdom I will have after passing to the afterlife is the wisdom I have accumulated throughout my existences. My moral development will be whatever level I will have achieved up to that point. My intellectual abilities will be those I have acquired during the evolutionary journey I—and you too— have embarked on from time immemorial. I might have access to latent knowledge I have acquired that is inaccessible now because of the limitation of my physical brain; but once free of it, I can tap it if needed. I might have certain mind powers compatible with the structure of the environment I will be gravitating to, all according to my level of development. I will have certain freedom of movement ungoverned by gravity. But I will become no more of a sage or saint when I *wake up* in the afterlife as I become every morning when I wake up from sleep. However, I will continue learning and growing even in the afterlife, for just as life, spiritual evolution never ends, regardless of the place we are manifesting.

We have seen in Rochelle's NDE account and others who tried to escape from pain through suicide that it does not work. Our happiness or unhappiness, our personal heaven or hell will follow us always, in this life or in the next. Killing the physical body will not end one's suffering or one's life. Death of the body changes only our mode of existence, from physical to non-physical, but will not change who or what we are.

A woman who also tried to end her problems by killing her body had this to say about her experience:

If you leave this life with a tormented soul, you will enter the next with a tormented soul.

Emmanuel, from his otherworldly perspective, shared the following about suicides as they enter the afterlife:

After death the first deception waiting for them is that the reality of (physical) life is not extinguished by the death of the physical body. Worse than that. It is exacerbated by appalling torments caused by their rebellious decision. There are suicides continuously feeling the (illusory) physical pains of the last earthly hour, as though they are still in the physical body. For years they feel the terrible impressions of the cause of physical death: the trajectory of the bullet that pierced the brain, the weight of the wheels that ran over them as they fled physical life, the silent waters passing over the dead body, or worse still, feeling and following minute by minute the decomposition of the physical body where it lay abandoned. Of all deviations of human life suicide is, perhaps, the greatest of all, for it is the absolute negation of the law of love and a supreme rebellion against the will of God...[5]

Drugs, a scourge that afflicts not only abusers but all those who love and care for those dependent on them, are another bridge to the hellish planes of the afterlife. Blessed are they who have the chance to return and mend their ways; for those staying due to overdose will bitterly regret it, but then it will be too late. And from those who have returned and told their story, we can learn not to make the same mistake.

Chapter 13

Overdose, a Hellish Trip

Sadira had been very depressed and wanted to die to escape her suffering. A nurse for many years working with cancer patients, she knew the right drugs and dosage needed to dive into eternal oblivion. That she knew; what she did not know was that life goes on and that we carry ourselves wherever we go. Be it in this life or in the next, we cannot escape from who we are and what we feel. We can change how we feel by changing how we think and act, but escaping we cannot.

I didn't care if I woke up or not. I didn't know why I was so depressed, but it was like I was saying: "God, I'm putting it in your hands." I don't know if I stopped breathing but I was (physically) unconscious.

What I saw was the most hideous, horrible thing! This was no nightmare! If you saw the movie *Ghost*, it was like where those horrible black things came out and were grabbing you. There were people screaming. It was unearthly voices, not earthly. It was horrible!

These things were all over me and they were screaming. I think I was naked there, because I remember feeling very ashamed. Everything was dark. I couldn't tell where the screaming was coming from. Then I actually saw these things, like horrible human beings, like anorexics. Their teeth were all ugly and twisted. The eyes were bulging. They were bald, no hair, and weren't wearing anything. They were naked! There must have been at least fifty, everywhere, and all around me. They were grabbing at my arms and my hair, and were screaming, pitiful screams, but not saying words. It was the type of moaning and screaming that you hear in a cancer ward, God forbid.

Then I saw them in my room, and I saw me in my room. Then I must have gone to a different plane, because then I could actually feel their breath next to me. They were wet, like sweaty, and they smelled so foul, like a rotting thing, like death. I've smelled dead rats which didn't smell as bad as this. Everything was just so vivid!

I felt judged. I felt that was my punishment. Those beings were there to punish me, but they didn't physically hurt me because I don't recall feeling pain. I just remember the pure terror! Then, slowly, the screaming started to get further away. It's like they were moving into another room to torture someone else.

Naturally, as Catholics, we're taught that we aren't supposed to take our own lives, because that means you've lost your faith in God. I can tell you this: there is no way I will ever think of attempting suicide ever again, or ever take that attitude. It was just so horrific! I went to hell! I went to hell! And I don't remember being redeemed! I don't remember any good part of it. I don't remember calling out for God and God rescuing me. I just remember waking up. We were taught that hell was a non-consuming fire, that it burns and hurts but doesn't actually burn the tissue. Personally, I never believed in hell. I believed that hell wasn't being able to see God. But after this, I believe in hell.

When I woke up I felt absolutely terrified, yet with a renewed hope. Suicide can never be the answer. This isn't an option. God doesn't want this. I believe in God very strongly. He will not excuse this. I saw hell!

I do a lot more for myself now. I used to be very dependent on my family. This experience did just totally changed my life. Now I'm glad it happened![1]

Sadira experienced hell and wisely decided she would not return there ever again.

Nothing Escapes Our Consciousness

Out of sight out of mind is not really a truism. Indelibly recorded in our mental body—a part of our spirit body which is also immortal and indestructible—is every memory of every deed we have done, not only in this life but in the many others we have been through. Even those little things we thought insignificant and do not seem to remember are still very alive somewhere in our extremely complex spirit body. Through the fine mesh of our stored memories emerge a very limited few which help us live our daily lives and perform the basic duties we came to this earth to perform. We could not lead a sane life if we had access to all we have been and done throughout our existences. To many of us just a small portion of what is happening in this life is already bad enough to drive us into despair, you can imagine if the floodgates of all our memories were open. Fortunately, merciful time lays a thin layer of dust on our old memories, allowing us to forget them for a while. But they never go away; they stay with us, alive, waiting to pop out when needed. Our memories may be hidden for a period, but they are never erased. Our consciousness is like a black hole: once a memory enters in, it cannot escape. And let us make no mistake, they will catch up with us, they will revisit us, giving us joy if they are pleasant and sorrow if otherwise. Either way they will serve a good purpose on our evolutionary path, for both will show us what we are passing or failing in the great school of life all of us are attending. They can help us grow faster if we learn what they are meant to teach us.

No Easy Way Out

Anita's heart stopped beating, her breathing ceased. She had overdosed. Her boyfriend found her unconscious and called police emergency. She was resuscitated and taken to a hospital, where she spent two weeks in intensive care on a respirator. As her body lay inert and torpid in the hospital bed, Anita, her true self, was sent to a crash course on the other side of life. And what she learned changed her life.

The first thing I remember was feeling like I was being restrained, like I couldn't move (onset of catalepsy as the spirit body is leaving), and there was no reason I couldn't move. I'm one of those people who cannot stand to be tied up. Finally, I did get loose and I know this will sound strange, but there were people walking around in what I thought were white uniforms. I thought I was on the deck of a cruise ship. I was trying to find my way out. Finally, I was able to break free, like from the upper part of my body.

The room I was in first was small and white. There wasn't anything there but a bed and a chair. I looked at myself. I was in the bed and I looked like hell. I broke free, first from the upper part of my body, and then I was walking through the corridors. That's when I saw my grandfather.

My grandfather had died about a year before. I told him I wanted to leave and he wouldn't let me. He was in a grumpy mood, which was always how he was. He was very stubborn. He said: "What the hell are you thinking? You're not going anywhere. Go back to your room." I thought this was very strange. He was wearing like a white robe, which wasn't his usual dress, and he was wearing a gray-blue shirt underneath and nothing on his feet. He was standing in front of a door to a room that I wanted to go into, but he wouldn't let me. Where I was it was cold and dark. The room I couldn't get into I knew was warm and had sunlight and sky. I knew the beach was there.

There was a man standing with my grandfather. He looked like Jesus Christ (prior to her NDE, Anita was an atheist), with long hair and a beard and mustache. He had on simple clothing and sandals on his feet. I didn't really confront Him at all, but I knew He was mad, though, because He was carrying the same expression as my grandfather, which was very disapproving. They weren't going to let me past them.

It was then that I saw everything that I ever did wrong. I was on trial. It was strange. I saw things that happened years and years ago that I couldn't even remember in my own consciousness. It was like they were judging. Any white lie or any little fib and stuff like that seemed to pop up. It was like anything mean that you ever did to somebody, whether you meant to hurt them or not, came up. You know, you may not consciously want to hurt somebody, but you do anyway. It was like a big broad sweep where I saw all the bad things I ever did. Honestly, it felt like I was in hell already. I felt like I was being judged for absolutely every single thing I had ever done. As far as what's right and wrong, I had been pretty clear on that, but I think everybody has the capability of telling little white lies. They're nothing that would seem to hurt anybody, but you hurt yourself in the long run.

After I saw all of that, my grandfather said I had to go back, and I knew I did if he said so. I remembered what his wrath could be like from when I was younger. I always trusted him, though. He was a good man even if he was grumpy. So I went back to my room. I felt alone in that room. I kept waiting, and it seemed like I waited forever. Then, finally, I felt restricted again (felt catalepsy as her spirit body approached the physical, prior to coinciding), and there I was back in my body.

Now I know I'm here for a purpose. I still don't know what it is, but this gave me a kick in the butt to tell me I'd better find out what I'm supposed to be doing on this fine planet. I guess if I'm going to be honest now, I'd better tell you that I was trying to take the easy way out. I am a fighter and I don't give up easily, but I was trying to give up.[2]

Finding a Purpose

I had not planned this section. As I write this paragraph, a new year has just begun. It is January 1st, 2013. Anita's life review prompted me to put everything aside for a moment, sit quietly and do my own life review. And there could be no better day than this. The New Year is a universal symbol of renewal and transformation, the perfect moment to heed the words of Paul, the Apostle of Christ, and "put off the old man... and be renewed in the spirit of your mind; and put on the new man, which after God is created in righteousness and true holiness."[3]

As I reflected on Anita's quest for the purpose in her life, I questioned about my own. I have been looking for it for years and years. Now I know the reason why it took me so long to find it. I was searching in the wrong place, *where it was not rather than where it was*, as a dear uncle used to joke. The old purpose I was looking for was something grand, something that could make a huge difference out there in the world, and that is *where it was not*. And *where is it?* Right here around me, in the little things I do every day; banal, they seem, but so important to the lives they touch.

It is first waking up every morning in thankfulness for the gift of being on this planet. It is walking to my little daughter's room every morning and waking her up with a gentle back rub; preparing her breakfast and getting her ready for school. It is praying to God for giving her and my older one protection, care, and love, for they are really His children, and blessed me with the opportunity to be their father in this life; He gave me His trust, and that I must honor; it's my duty. It is making sure that they are safe, loved, and cared for.

It is going downstairs and replenishing our cats' food and water; they come running as they see me there; they're hungry and thirsty and know they will be filled; it is even cleaning their litter boxes so they find them nice and tidy when nature calls; they are also God's creatures under my care; and that I must honor.

My purpose is doing the little everyday things that keep me and those I care for and those I can somehow touch going forward, and finding joy in doing them. It is doing positive things that enrich my own existence and those around me. It is doing to others what I would like done to me, as Jesus said, "for this is the law and the prophets."[4] Nothing spectacular, nothing world shattering, just the basics for a happy and healthy daily survival on this planet of trials and tribulations. But enough to stand before the Being of Light and answer with a clear consciousness when He asks, "What have you done with your life to show me?" "I have done the best I could with the resources I had; I lived by Your laws, and You are my witness."

With the exception of Brad Barrows' NDE in Chapter 10, all the others we have seen were experienced by adults. Now we are going to see some extraordinary experiences by children, which, just like the ones reported by adults, corroborate that death of the physical body is not the end of our existence. If you or a loved one have gone through the horrific emotional pain of (physically) losing a child, the following cases may give you comfort. You will see that not only she or he continues to exist, but has also been cared for and guided from the moment she or he left physical life. And the caretakers may well be the very ones who loved and cared for them while in physical life.

Chapter 14

Children Near Death

Looking at Katie she was a typical nine-year old American girl — pretty, long blonde hair, a bit shy at first but pleasantly lively once she felt comfortable with you. What was different about her was that she, just a few days before, had been found floating unconscious in a YMCA swimming pool. How long she had been there, minutes or hours, has never been determined.

What had been determined as emergency room personnel assessed her condition was that her chances of physical survival were slim, ten percent, if lucky. Dr. Melvin Morse, the physician in charge of the ER, had even allowed her family to hold a prayer vigil around her bed, since "she was going to die anyway."[1] Physically die, we all will, but when our turn comes, and that time was not Katie's. Three days later, when she woke up from a coma, she was fully recovered.

Dr. Morse had scheduled a follow-up visit to talk with Katie to find out what had happened. How she had fallen into the pool — by accident, a seizure, someone pushed her? This information was important to determine the course of treatment, namely if it had been a seizure. Katie, brought in by her mom, sat in a room waiting for Dr. Morse to come and exam her for the first time since her miraculous recovery. Dr. Morse knew Katie; he had worked diligently to save her life; he had seen her very closely during those long minutes on the emergency table. But Katie had never seen Dr. Morse; she had drowned and her brain was too swollen for consciousness when she was brought in to the hospital. But recognize him she did, the minute he came in.

"Hello, Katie! I'm Doctor Morse. How are you feeling?"

Turning to her mother, Katie said, "That's the one with the beard. First there was this tall doctor (Dr. Bill Longhurst) who did not have a beard, and then he (Dr. Morse) came in."

This information would be enough to baffle the skeptical resident doctor, but Katie had more to say about what she saw when, according to brain science, she could not have seen. As Katie spoke and Morse listened, he began to feel crinkles forming on the smooth surface of his skepticism.

"First I was in the big room, and then they moved me to a smaller room where they did X-rays on me."

Among other accurate details, she said she had a tube inserted up her nose. Dr. Morse, whose experience with Katie turned him into a pioneer of children's NDE research, was amazed at the accuracy of the details she gave, "Even though her eyes had been closed and she had been profoundly comatose during the entire experience."[2]

For medical reasons, Dr. Morse wanted to know what caused her drowning, and asked, "What do you remember about being in the swimming pool?" The answer he received was not what he was expecting.

"Do you mean when I visited the Heavenly Father?" Katie answered. It was now the doctor's turn to take a deep breath.

"Well, that's a good place to start. Tell me about meeting the Heavenly Father."

"I met Jesus and the Heavenly Father." And that was all she said during that visit. Not that she did not have more to say, but perhaps the look on the doctor's face scared her, so she stopped for the day.

In his skepticism, Dr. Morse noticed not only crinkles, but now also fissures and cracks. He wanted to know more of what Katie had to say, and scheduled another visit. In this visit, the fissures and cracks gave way to cliffs and splits. His skepticism was wavering, and by the end of the visit, he was a changed man.

"She remembered nothing about the drowning itself. Her first memory was of darkness and the feeling that she was so heavy she could not move." (This happens when the spirit body is already out, but so close to the physical that physical sensations are still perceived.)

"What happened next?" he asked.

"There was a tunnel, and Elizabeth was at the entrance."

Katie did not know who or what Elizabeth was, describing her as tall and nice with golden hair. Elizabeth accompanied Katie through the tunnel, and upon reaching the end, the girl met her (physically) deceased grandfather, and several other people as well. Katie was introduced to two children, Andy and Mark, who were "waiting to be born", with whom she played while there and through whom she met many other people.[3]

Dr. Morse listened to Katie's heavenly stroll with wonder and great intensity, taking in every detail of her otherworldly adventure. But as spectacular as it might have been, this, of course, was unverifiable information. But the verifiable information would come next, and that was when Morse's wavering skepticism crumbled to dust.

When our loved ones leave earthly life, we, the left-behinds, dressed in our gross physical body cannot cross over to the other side to visit them at will. We can, and we do, but when the physical body is asleep and we, as spirit that we are, leave it for a spell. However, when we are on the other side of life we can, and we will, return to earth for various purposes. Our new body allows for that, though we will not be able to interact with physical things, but come over for a visit we can.

"Would you like to visit your family in your house?" asked Elizabeth.

"Yes," said Katie.

Katie came and took a floating stroll through her house. She visited her brothers and sisters as they played with their toys. One of the brothers was playing with his GI Joe doll, taking it for a ride in a toy jeep. A sister played with her Barbie doll. With hearing unimpaired even if her body was comatose in the hospital miles away, Katie heard her sister singing a popular rock song of the time. Having seen her siblings, she drifted through the house looking for her mom, and found her in the kitchen preparing a meal. Katie glanced at the living room; on the couch she saw her father, sitting quietly, worried about the (bodily) health of his precious daughter, comatose in the hospital.

But Katie had seen more than that—the clothes her loved ones were wearing, their positions and movements in the house, even the food her mom was cooking—rice and roast chicken. When Katie told her flabbergasted parents and siblings later, they confirmed the details she had given during her invisible home visit.

From there Elizabeth took Katie to see the Heavenly Father and Jesus, and Katie was asked if she wanted to go back home with her family. Crying, she said that she wanted to stay with them in heaven.

"Don't you want to see your mother again?" asked Jesus.

"Yes," Katie replied.

That said, Katie awoke in her physical body, returning to earth to complete her allotted time.

"What did you think of heaven?" asked Dr. Morse.

"Heaven is fun, you will see."[4]

Astonished by Katie's experience, Dr. Morse went on a quest for other children who had been near death and might have had similar experiences. He designed quite an interesting experiment. He wanted to know if children with serious illnesses who had not been in the eminence of death also reported NDE episodes. He had no problem identifying 121 critically ill children and teenagers, but none facing the risk of dying. These children had been on respirators, and had been treated with tranquilizers and narcotics. But found only twelve who had been near death. These twelve children had suffered cardiac arrests caused by drowning, car accidents, kidney diseases, asthma and other heart problems. He was even more astonished when he found out the results. None of the 121 patients reported episodes akin to NDEs, while the majority of the twelve children who had been near death—consistent with PMH Atwater's ratio—did. Some reported extraordinary full-blown NDEs, while others had partial, but by no means less intense experiences.

Dr. Morse studied NDEs of American children; in England, Sam Parnia, the doctor who wants to create medications to produce NDE effects, also found children who had had NDEs. Like adult NDErs, the experiences of children are consistent all over the world. The following is an amazing account of a case investigated by Dr. Parnia, with verifiable elements proving that not only we do survive bodily death, but we might also stick around to help loved ones when needed.

The Floating Lady

My son Andrew, then three and a half years old, was admitted to hospital with a heart problem... He had to undergo open-heart surgery. About two weeks after the surgery, he started asking when he could go back to the beautiful sunny place with all the flowers and animals. I said, "We'll go to the park in a few days when you're feeling better." "No," he said, "I don't mean the park, I mean the sunny place I went with the lady." I asked him, "What lady?" and he said, "The lady that floats." I told him I didn't know what he meant, and that I must have forgotten where the sunny place was, and he said, "You didn't take me there. The lady came and got me. She held my hand and we floated up... You were outside when I was having my heart mended... It was okay. The lady looked after me; the lady loves me. It wasn't scary; it was lovely. Everything was bright and colorful, [but] I wanted to come back to see you."' I asked him, "When you came back, were you asleep or awake or dreaming?" and he said, "I was awake, but I was up on the ceiling, and when I looked down I was lying in a bed with my arms by my sides, and doctors were doing something to my chest. Everything was really bright, and I floated back down..."

About a year after his operation, we were watching [the TV show] *Children's Hospital* and a child was having heart surgery. Andrew got excited and said, "I had that machine" [a bypass machine]. I said, "I don't think you did. " He said, "Yes, I did, really." "But," I said, "you were asleep when you had your operation, so you wouldn't have seen any machines." He said, "I know I was asleep, but I could see it when I was looking down." I said, "If you were asleep, how could you be looking down?" He said, "You know, I told you, when I floated up with the lady..."

[One day] I showed him a photo of my [deceased mother] when she was my age now, and he said, "That's her. That's the lady."[5]

If there is something capable of touching one's soul deeply it is the death of a child. A child is supposed to be able to grow to adulthood, to have dreams, to fulfill those dreams, not dying before any of that happens. One aspect of my afterlife research that fascinated me the most, both in my NDE studies and when a child is dying, is the *support* she or he receives from the other side of life, and in a great number of cases from their physically dead but spiritually alive grandparents. Remember the Brazilian boy and his *imaginary* friend Paulinho? Just like Andrew in the account above, he had never met his grandfather in physical life; and both Andrew and the Brazilian boy recognized the grandparents from family photos, and their appearance matched their last human incarnation. Accounts of physically dead grandparents and other close relatives coming down to earth to help their physically alive (or we could say spiritually dead) loved ones are rife in angelic intervention literature.[6]

The ties of love (or hate) we have with those around us— family members, close friends, business associates and others—

are not new and very few from this present lifetime. The stronger these ties are, the closer we are with those bound by them; ties that are seldom broken, either while we are together in this life or when one of us moves over to the other side. And from the other side of life, we will watch over those who have been put under our care. All of us, the entire human race, are evolutionary partners who have come to earth in search of spiritual progress, even if now we have no clue about it. And the closer our relationships with these partners, the greater our commitment with each other to help each other in this extraordinary journey, even if we are not aware of it.

There is nothing supernatural about a physically dead grandmother coming down to earth to watch over her little grandson as he undergoes a serious operation; or coming to escort a granddaughter back to the spiritual world as her time on earth has ended; or a loving grandfather coming down to play with his lonely grandson. This is love in action! It is love doing what it does best—healing, consoling, uplifting hope—and for that it transcends ages, distances, even realities. For love, the breath of God, is the tenacious glue that holds life tightly together.

All of us when living either the physical or the spiritual life are on different levels of evolution compared to each other. You certainly remember in your classes those schoolmates who breezed through the toughest subjects—calculus, chemistry, physics—while others could not ever get it. Not because they did not want to understand; despite their efforts, somehow they just could not. Among your schoolmates were also those always willing to lend a hand when you got stuck on a problem. There were those funny ones it was so pleasant to be around; those who offered you a share of their lunch; those who stole your lunch for fun; those who uplifted your mood when you were down; and those who dragged you down when they saw you happy; those who loved to make you laugh, and those who delighted in making you cry.

You can clearly see such distinctions now among your own family members, friends, fellow workers, neighbors, and other people you associate with. What we are and the way we act are in direct relation with the level of progress—morally, intellectually, and spiritually—we have achieved throughout our existences. The final goal of each and every one of us, even if today we are on the other side of the evolutionary tracks, is to achieve a level of progress in which everything we do enriches and empowers someone else's life. And for the achievers of this level, there is no reward greater than what they receive, even if never asked for—an ineffable sense of being an active part in the works of creation, seeding love and spreading joy everywhere they pass by.

While many have already achieved such a level, sadly, many still lag far behind, causing hurt and ruin to the lives of those they are meant to care for and to protect. But when humans hurt, angels heal. The hurt we suffer from others can teach us to forgive, and the care we receive from angels can teach us to love—the two main lessons we are on this earth to learn.

When Angels Lend a Hand

Laura was three and half years old when she had a near-death experience:

> My father, in a blind drunken rage, raped and sodomized and beat me to death in the middle of the night. At the most extreme outpost of pain, I cried out to God and in that moment I was torn from (physical) life. As I died I felt myself raised up by angels in robes of many colors. I didn't know where they were taking me as they flew, carrying me up higher and higher in the sky. Finally, we reached a place where emptiness gave way to form, and form took the shape of huge cloudlike masses on which other angels seemed to be

walking, although they too floated through the air. The angels carrying me lay me at the feet of a beautiful female angel whose radiating love was more powerful than any of those around her. She said to me in a voice whose sweetness and tone are unknown on earth, "Tell me your story." I said to her, not in spoken words but in thoughts, "I will, but now I need to rest." My spirit had no energy, even to answer this loving lady. God in the manifestation of infinite light appeared off to my left, and I was engulfed in a form of all-powerful, all-nourishing love. That divine being appeared as a massive column of golden light, with the suggestion of a human shape inside. I both saw and felt his light, feeling as if I were in a warm bath that completely healed and protected me. I never wanted to leave. No conversation passed between us, but in those infinite moments I acquired the knowledge that allowed me to go back to earth to complete my life. After this infinite moment had passed, there began a battle for my life between the angels in heaven and the doctors on earth. Every time the doctors pounded on my chest, my spirit was sucked into my body for a split second, only to be pulled back again by the angels. They held me by my feet, struggling to keep me from coming back. Finally, the doctors pounded one last time. I heard an angel say, "They're stronger than we are," and I was sucked back into my body, sat up, screamed, and passed out. To this day, I always have the feeling that I need to go back, that there was something more I was meant to do there before returning. That feeling of incompleteness keeps me half in the other world all the time.[7]

Lessons Learned

Laura had to undergo surgery for the damage her father's abuse caused her. She summarized the lessons she learned from both the abuse and her NDE thus:

I learned how to live with my murderer for another fifteen years by learning what I could from him and leaving the rest. I learned that the most important phenomena in the universe are love, truth, and the quest for knowledge. I received a clear sense of my purpose in life and how I must achieve it. I was given the gift of foreseeing things before they happen and the ability to visualize events, images and forms, and then bring them into being. I learned that we are wounded, and heal from deep wounds, not so that we may somehow be safe forever, but so that we may be wounded again in a new way. Most of all, I acquired a deep love of death and a longing to be in the presence of God again, a longing that is with me every moment of every day. It is only for the knowledge of His presence that I am able to live.[8]

What Children Learn from NDE

Dr. Melvin Morse followed up for several years the children he had studied who had undergone NDE. He checked both their physical and mental development through the years. An outstanding characteristic he found was a marked increase in the feeling of empathy. Empathy is the ability of a person to identify with or feel what another person is feeling, to stand in their shoes so to speak. It is the capacity to feel someone else's pain and sorrow as if they were one's own. Empathy is a characteristic present in people high up in the spiritual development scale; it is one of the main virtues in the development of compassion. It was empathy which prompted Siddhartha Gautama, the Buddha; Jesus Christ; Saint Francis of Assisi; Mahatma Gandhi; Mother Teresa of Calcutta and thousands of other anonymous enlightened souls throughout the world to devote their lives working to alleviate human suffering.

Dr. Morse discovered that many NDE children in his group, as is common with adult NDErs as well, were involved in some kind of charitable work to promote the well-being of people and/or their community. They were engaged in these activities part-time or full-time, either as volunteers or professionally. Dr. Morse also discovered that these children grew up more spiritualized and more balanced physically and mentally. Their eating habits were healthier; they showed greater maturity and did better in school when compared to children within the same age group who did not have NDE. As is also common in adult NDErs, many NDE children also developed psychic abilities. Katie, for instance, the fascinating case we saw in the beginning of this chapter and whose experience changed Dr. Morse's life, said she could see people's auras, the energy field emanating from every living organism. Others told him they could see and talk to discarnate spirits, an ability known as mediumship, like the woman who conjured up Samuel to give advice to King Saul.

Another peculiarity Dr. Morse found was that his NDE children grew up with a sense of universal cosmic connection to all things (cosmic consciousness), while other children (and an immense number of adults!) barely know what it means. As we learned from Laura, they also feel they have a purpose in life and live their earthly existence knowing (not believing!) that the death of the body is not the end of their existence. They trust their intuition and feel they can always connect to that divine presence which welcomed and guided them during their experience, but without the need of having another NDE. "If you have seen the light on the other side once," a NDE child told Dr. Morse, "you can see it again if you try. It is always with you."[9]

Learning in the Beyond, a Fascinating Story

Lynn was eleven years old when she drowned. Leaving her body, she caught a glimpse of the other side of life, and returned to tell what happened:

My brother and I went swimming. He had a problem. I tried to get him out of the water, but in his panic he pulled me under several times. We both drowned. He died and I came back. I can remember it all like yesterday. Just as I could no longer stay afloat, a strange sound like ringing in my ears started. A peaceful feeling came over me. I felt my spirit come out of my body and I went into a black void. That was a little frightening. A long way off there was a pinprick of light. I moved toward it, slowly at first, then faster and faster as if I were on top of a train accelerating. Then I stopped and stepped fully into the light. I noticed everything—sky, buildings, glass—emitted its own light. And everything was much more colorful than what we see here. A river meandered around. On the other side was a city, and a road running through it to another city, and another city, and another and another. Right in front of me but across the river were three men. They projected themselves to me. They didn't walk or fly; they projected over. I didn't recognize them, yet I knew one was Lynn Bib. (I was named after him. He died a matter of weeks before I was born.) I knew these three men were looking out for me, like a welcoming committee to escort me over the river to the first city. I had the feeling that if I went with them, there would be no coming back, so I hesitated. The first city was like the first grade. People stayed there until they were ready to go to the next city, an eternal progression, from city to city. Behind me and to the left was a strong light source, very brilliant and filled with love. I knew it was a person. I called it God for lack of a better term. I could not see it; I felt what seemed like a male presence. He communicated to me, not so much in words but telepathically, and he asked, "Why did you hesitate?" I replied, "Well, I'm kind of young to die." He chuckled. "We have babies die." I said, "Well, there are some things I want to know first." He replied, "What do you want to know?" "What is death?" I asked. He said, "Turn and look to one side." As I did, I saw a bad car wreck. Several people had been killed. Out of some of the

bodies a spirit came up to progress on. Some who didn't
believe it was possible stayed in their bodies and wouldn't
emerge. I asked if they could be reached and he said, "Yes,
some more quickly than others and some maybe never."
Death, then, is not believing anything. I asked, "What is hell?"
He said, "Turn and look again." I saw an old woman in a
rocking chair determined to sit and rock and worry about
children and grandchildren and everything else. Hell is
therefore a lack of wisdom and not moving on, choosing not
to go any further, sitting there and doing nothing. Hell is not
a place. I asked if there was a Devil or Satan. He said to me,
"Would God allow that?" He continued, "If I made you God
for just a few seconds, what would you do first?" I knew my
first act would be to eliminate any Devil or Satan. I asked,
"How do I know right from wrong?" He replied, "Right is
helping and being kind. Wrong is not only hurting but not
helping when you can." We walked as I asked about the
universe and reasons for everything. All of these things were
shown to me. Then he wondered if I still wanted to return to
the physical world. "I do want to return." He asked, "Why?" I
said I would help my mother whom my father had left with
four children and one on the way. God kind of chuckled and
asked me for the real reason. I said I would leave the earth a
little better than I found it. "Then you may return with some
knowledge of things you have learned, but the rest will be
veiled for a time. Live in such way that you will not feel bad
when you return here again." I woke up face down in the mud
of the river bottom and was *lifted* to the top. I threw up great
amounts of water, and then pulled myself out of the river only
to discover that my brother had died.[10]

Though I have been saying that we die when it is our time to die,
not before or after, it seems possible there can be 'adjustments'
along the way. And our sojourn here may be prolonged or

shortened, according to circumstances. My own experience may have been a case in point. So let us see how we might cheat the Grim Reaper for a while.

Chapter 15

Cheating the Grim Reaper?

When you are poor and live out in the boonies, you need to be creative to survive. When a can of tomato sauce—if you can afford one—runs out, for instance, you do not just throw it away, you wash it, smooth out the sharp edges, and it becomes a drinking cup; chicken feathers and corn husks become fillings for homemade pillows and mattresses. If you have small fussy children in need of appeasement and have no toys and no TV, give them pots and pans to bang on and you calm them down. That was my mom's strategy to keep me distracted, and a certain cooking pot became my favorite, as my mom told me later.

She also told me that I was eleven months old when I got out of my crib by myself for the first time. However, she did not see my prowess that morning. When she saw me I was nearly dead. That morning she had gone to the stream nearby to wash clothes. And my favorite toy, an aluminum pot, was doing the job for which it was created; it was sitting on the hot wood-burning stove, filled with boiling beans my mom was preparing for the day's meal. I went straight for it, grabbed the handle and poured all the contents on me. When she came in I was sitting motionless on the dirt floor. She took off my shirt and chunks of cooked flesh came stuck to the fabric; she could even see the bone on my chest. It took several hours to reach the closest hospital, and when the doctor saw my condition he told my parents to prepare my funeral.

My mom was an unschooled teenager, nineteen years old then. "That's for God to decide," she told the doctor. "You go on and do your job. He's not going to die."

From that moment on she prayed unceasingly for my survival, and after several days my health began to improve. I was her firstborn, and we talked about this episode many times as I grew up. She would always say with unwavering certainty, "I couldn't let you die."

Whether I—my body, that is—cheated the Grim Reaper then is hard to tell. But many are the cases in the death and dying literature where patients defy medical prognosis that they are terminal and live much longer than expected, even in extremely frail health.

Revisiting Celi's experience... As I mentioned in the beginning of the book, she had three close calls with death during her hospital stay. Not only her family had been called to say their goodbyes, but also the priest to administer the Sacrament of the Sick, as she was about to depart earthly existence. During my interview with her I asked if she saw medical personnel coming in and out of the ICU while she was out of her body. She said she did. And as I have mentioned, she would even step out of their way. Knowing that there is constant influence from the spiritual side of life on our side, especially in hospitals, I asked her if she had seen anything unusual in the ICU in addition to what she had already told me.

She was silent for a moment, then said, "There were people there."

"Hospital people?" I asked.

"No, different people."

"What kind of people?"

She chuckled again, then said, "Like not from here."

"From Jaú?" I prodded.

"No, from earth."

"Oh," I said, feigning surprise, "Spirits, maybe?"

I heard a sigh of relief, as though she needed to let it out and was pleased she had.

"Yes."

"How many?" I asked.

"Four."

"What gender?"

"Three men and one woman."

"Did you talk to them?"

"No, but they talked among themselves."

"Could you capture what they were talking about?"

"Not everything, but they talked about the body. They seemed concerned about the body."

I asked her to describe them. She said they looked middle-aged, gray-haired and wearing white silky-like robes. These entities were constantly present in the ICU, giving their full attention to the physical body. When medical personnel came in to check on her body, the spirit beings would surround them.

Celi was the main breadwinner of her family; a young adult son was sort of going astray; and another daughter was having serious personal issues. Celi, an extremely caring mother who had her first daughter at age 15, was the type of person who would invoke all the cosmic forces to help her survive to guide her family. And certainly her pleas were heard and even angels had been sent to work their miracles on her. She was given more time on earth, enough to assure that her beloved children would be cared for and guided if she would go. "Some dying people realize they will die more peacefully under certain conditions; until those conditions are met, they may delay the timing of their death."[1] For the next two years Celi lived in excruciating pain. When I met her another time, she told me, "I'm ready now." Shortly after, the infection returned, worse than before; and this time it could not be controlled. Celi's time came when she was ready, and having finished her earthly work, peacefully she went.

When you read the lives of certain historical figures, it seems some souls come to earth with specific missions at certain crucial times. They either come to promote a quantum leap in human progress or to eliminate hurdles that are preventing a speedier flow in progress, and once finished, they leave. Jesus, for instance, left earth as soon as He had taught what He needed to teach in order to promote the necessary quantum leap, the greatest ever in the history of humanity until now. Abraham Lincoln after abolishing slavery and just three months after he assured the passing of the Thirteenth Amendment, which legally outlawed slavery. Mahatma Gandhi, five months after India gained independence from the British—33 years after he had begun his peaceful crusade to free his country. And Martin Luther King Jr. just a week before President Lyndon Johnson signed the Civil Rights Act of 1968, which, along with the Act of 1964, signed as a result of King's campaign, outlawed racial discrimination. Thus completing his earthly work, King moved on to the other side of life.

On the other hand, would it be possible if such missionaries shirked their assigned duty they could return home earlier than planned? Apparently it would.

The great Brazilian medium Francisco Xavier started talking to spirits, his deceased mother being the first one, when he was five years old. He died in 2002, at age ninety-two, by which time he had channeled four-hundred-and-twelve books dictated by a number of discarnate spirits. Emmanuel was his spirit guide and the coordinator of Xavier's writing work. Xavier worked long hours every day of the week, never married, never received money for his extensive spiritual and humanitarian work, lived an incredibly simple life, and was nearly blind in one eye. He was sought by, and gave the same caring attention to, everyone who approached him for guidance, from the destitute to celebrities to presidents of the country. He was known in Brazil as "the man called love". When he was fifty-nine years old he finished channeling the hundredth book. He told Emmanuel that he was tired and asked if it might be possible to stop writing and do something else instead.

Emmanuel told him that everyone has free will and every

one's free will must be respected, and that indeed Xavier could stop writing. However, he said, your mission in this life is to write books to console people and to instruct them about the afterlife; that's what you came here for. If you stop writing, which you have the right to, there is no more reason for you to stay on earth. "Do you want to stop writing?" Obviously, Xavier knew what Emmanuel meant, and although Xavier knew he would continue living if he left earthly life, he preferred to stay. "We shall continue writing books," he assured his guide, and did so for the next thirty years.

Sadly, suicides leave earth before their allotted time, an action they will regret. But thanks to the mercifulness of our loving Creator and the help of enlightened spirits they are helped and guided. And in time they will repair their mistake and will keep working on their spiritual evolution, just as everyone of us will.

When it Isn't Time to Go

That night (in her spirit body) I was picked up, unwillingly, by a lady wearing a long, green, flowing robe, medieval-style. She carried me in her arms down a long, dark, green-moldy type dirt-walled tunnel, swiftly taking me somewhere I did not want to go. She mind-talked to me and kept trying to explain that I had to go, and nothing could prevent it, no matter how much I didn't want to leave. I think that was why she was carrying me, for I know I would have run back down the tunnel otherwise.

Suddenly she heard bells bonging from very far, very far away. She stopped and turned to listen. She told me there had been a change and I had to go back after all. She had no compassion during all of this, simply a formal, strong approach towards me. Then she carried me back to my bed and placed me on it, still drawn up in a contracted bundle from being carried so long. I called out to her, but she rapidly walked away into the tunnel.

When my mother rushed in and heard my jabbered story—which scared me more than any dream—she became terrified due to my fragile condition.[2]

(This report was by a paramedic instructor who had a NDE at age six, during a bout of measles.)

When it Is Time to Go

From the very first moment we come into this life, there is only one certain thing we can count on—one day, sooner for some and later for others—the physical body we are wearing will die. Though we all know this is true, it is a reality not very easily dealt with. If it is difficult to accept the death of adults, you can imagine that of a child who has just sprung to life. Parents of terminally ill children, for instance, desperately want them to remain on earth. Even though their children are suffering and ready to leave physical life, parents could be doing more harm than good by wanting their children to stay. Giving permission to leave this life and praying for a peaceful passing could be more beneficial than praying for them to stay. And the spirit, knowing that it is time to leave this life but is being held back by loving and caring parents, may have to be creative to deliver a message for acceptance so they can return to the spiritual realm.

In his book *Closer to the Light*, Dr. Melvin Morse tells of a five-year-old boy who was dying from a malignant brain tumor. He had been in a coma for three weeks, and his family had stayed in his room praying, day and night, for the boy to recover. By the end of the third week the pastor of their church went to the boy's hospital room and told his parents an extraordinary story.

"I had a dream," he said, "that he appeared to me and said, 'It's my time to die. You must tell my parents to quit praying. I am supposed to go now.'"

The pastor hesitated to deliver the message, but it had been so vivid that it was hard to ignore. "It's as though he was right there in the room, talking to me face to face," he told the boy's parents.

The parents finally accepted the pastor's dream as being a message from their son, and began to pray for a peaceful transition. Caressing his comatose body, they told him he would be terribly missed, but he had permission to leave if that was his destiny. Suddenly, the boy awoke from his coma. He thanked his family for letting him go, and told them his death was near. He died the following day.

The mother I will be referring to in the next account shared a case with me which she witnessed. Her hemophiliac four-year-old son contaminated with HIV virus shared a hospital room with another boy with the same condition and about the same age; both were terminally ill. The mother of this other boy was a fervent Christian. She would stay in the room reading the Bible and praying for her son's recovery, unrelentingly and untiringly. At one point the boy begged his mother to stop reading the Bible and praying because she was making it very difficult. She did not understand what he meant and he did not elaborate on it. But to please her son she stopped and stepped outside. When she returned a few moments later, the boy had made his transition.

Dying Children Know Life Goes On

For clarity's sake, I am going to repeat what Emmanuel said regarding children. "Up to seven years of age, the (incarnated) spirit is still in the adaptation phase to the new existence it came to earth to experience. Up to this age the integration (of the spirit element) and organic matter (the material body) is not yet perfected."[3] This imperfect integration of spirit and body allows children to straddle realities—they live in the physical world but are still somewhat connected with the spiritual realm, even if subconsciously. When a serious illness strikes and debilitates their already fragile body, the connection with the spiritual realm strengthens, and they become more attuned to their spiritual origin. At this point it becomes clear to them that earthly life is temporary and they will continue their existence after the death of the physical body. So clear and so certain is this fact to them that you often see them—the little children—consoling their parents regarding their impending death. Death and dying literature and real-life experiences are replete with such cases.

Some twenty-five years ago, blood screening for donation in Brazil was not that sophisticated. At the height of the AIDS epidemic, there were many cases of donated blood contaminated with the HIV virus. About that time in Brazil the main treatment of hemophilia (a genetic bleeding disorder) was blood transfusion, and many hemophiliac children acquired AIDS as a consequence. One of those children was the son of the woman who shared the previous case with me. From her I have personally heard one of the most beautiful stories I have ever known about a dying child.

Her son was contaminated with the HIV virus when he was one year of age. From the time she found out, she began a daily struggle to save her son's life. When her son was about three and understood what was going on, he began to tell his mother to take it easy, that he was going to die and there was nothing wrong with it and nothing was going to prevent it from happening. Every time he saw her sad or crying he would come up to console her. As his health worsened, his mother became more desperate. When he was four she made a doctor's appointment to inquire about the possibility of some novel treatment that might have been developed which could save her son's life. Upon listening to his mother's plea, the boy told the doctor with astonishing calm for the doctor to tell his mother that he was dying and there was nothing to be done. As the (physical) death of her son approached, the mother's anguish skyrocketed. In the hospital a few days before passing, he told his mother that he was going to show her where he was about to go so she would not be so sad. A few minutes before his transition, the mother began to feel a strange sensation throughout her body; first like dizziness, then her body became heavy and her eyes refused to stay open. She lay down on a couch in the room, beside her son's bed. She felt herself leaving the body, was surrounded by an intense darkness, then saw a source of light, which increased and she noticed it was the entrance of a tunnel. As the light expanded, she saw on the other side a group of discarnate spirits waiting for her son. She then awoke from her trance; there was a commotion around her son's bed, he had just left his body. Prior to that, when his father came to visit, crying profusely for his son's impending death, the boy said to him, "Daddy, don't cry for me because I will never die."

You noticed from the mother's experience the same initial pattern of a NDE—sensation of leaving the body, darkness, source of light, tunnel and spiritual realm. Her son was going to follow the same path as NDErs report; however, as opposed to NDERs who return, the boy was going to stay, since it *was* his time to die.

Shared death experience,[4] also coined by Dr. Raymond Moody, is the term that describes the phenomenon the mother vicariously experienced. As the world population increases and more people die daily, such experiences have been commonly reported by family members and friends sitting by a loved one's deathbed. When Hamlet told Horatio there were more things in heaven and earth than dreamt of in his philosophy, he was right. There are in the world today so many phenomena verifying the continuity of life after bodily death that no scientific theory claiming otherwise can stand against. All we need, as Jesus has said, are eyes that can see and ears that can hear, and an open and flexible mind capable of expanding so that we can fit in it all the mysteries that surround us.

And one of these mysteries is our own nature which appears

to be just physical, but in reality it is not so. For appearances can be deceiving, and even though we see and may be aware of our material nature only, deeper within each one of us is the spiritual, our true immortal essence.

Chapter 16

Our Double Nature

Have you ever heard of Charles Darwin? Of course you have, who has not? This is the naturalist whose theory of evolution by natural selection prevails in the scientific community and academia worldwide since he launched his book *On the Origin of Species*, in 1859.

In Darwinian evolution theory, life happened by chance, by a fluke of nature. This fluke created "the first living cell, about four billion years ago,"[1] from which every living thing on this planet, from that time to the present, descended—from bacteria, to mahogany, to dinosaurs, to grasshoppers, to you and me. According to Darwinism, every species that ever existed and exists today is a product of this fluke, created from a random accident in the DNA structure of cells called *mutation*. "... [M]utations that are simply errors in the copying process [of cells],"[2] as simple as that.

Webster Dictionary defines *error* as a deviation from a standard or specification, also as a deficiency or imperfection in structure or function, or in the outcome of something. When you set on your kitchen counter the recipe of that mouth-watering cherry pie only you can bake, you know that if you err on the quantity of certain key ingredients, you are likely to ruin it. You know that your error will cause imperfection to your creation. You would not expect, for instance, that rather than baking a ruined cherry pie your mistake would produce a scrumptious cheesecake. However, in Darwinism, genetic errors—a fluke of nature—says the theory, created miracles, not only simple bacteria but marvelous organisms such as corals and fishes in the ocean. If a pharmacist errs on the percentage of certain key ingredients of a medication, he cannot expect his mistake to endow the patient with additional health, but ruin it and perhaps even kill rather than cure the patient. But in Darwinism, genetic errors produced other marvels; rather than deviating from a standard, errors created trees, flowers, and vegetables. If a builder errs when mixing the correct quantity of key ingredients to lay the foundation of an edifice, or uses inadequate-sized steel bars to support its structure, he cannot expect his mistake to produce a better edifice, but an imperfect one. In Darwinism, when genes erred they produced not imperfections, but awe-striking creations such as birds, animals, humans and all other living things that ever existed.

Apparently, however, such overwhelming random genetic errors that created wonders belong to the remote past. Today genetic errors create diseases and malformation, rather than marvelous and perfect new species. It seems like nature somehow has corrected itself since then, and flukes have run their course. For quite a while now sea creatures no longer leave the oceans to become land creatures; and gators are still hatching gators; baby whales are still the species emerging from their mother's womb; flamingos still hatch flamingos; tigers continue to bring forth tiger offspring; apes never again descended from the trees and walked upright.

Back to your culinary artistry, you know that to bake a cupcake, even the tiniest one to enter the Guinness World Records, you need a bit of flour, a few drops of water, and a smidgen of sugar, at least. If you put nothing in the baking cup, nothing will emerge out of it. Yet, in Darwinian, materialistic view nothingness created not only our universe but "everything that was, that is, and will be"[3]—even though it cannot create the tiniest cupcake.

The Heretic Scientist

So you know who Charles Darwin was. Now, have you ever heard of Alfred Russell Wallace? You might or might not. Wallace was also British and a brilliant naturalist, fourteen years younger than Darwin. He had worked out, independently, a theory of natural selection, like Darwin's. Darwin knew of Wallace's work and even co-published a paper on the subject with him, in 1858. In fact, it was Wallace who prompted Darwin to finish and publish his theory on the origin of species after more than twenty years of wait, lest Wallace published his first. "I have more especially been induced to do this (publish the book)," wrote Darwin, "as Mr. Wallace, who is now studying the natural history of the Malay Archipelago, has arrived at almost exactly the same general conclusions that I have on the origin of species."[4]

Like Darwin, Wallace also believed that living organisms evolved from lower forms, and adapted to the environment they lived in, developing or discarding biological traits in order to survive and grow in that environment. According to evolution theory, we, humans, are ancient African apes who learned to walk on two legs. As our legs became stronger, we left the African jungles and spread throughout the world. "Homo erectus (upright man) carried out the first grand migration of people by moving out of Africa, first throughout the Asian world and then throughout southern and western Europe."[5] As we treaded the earth for countless years we discarded a lot of unneeded hair, and became different from our ape ancestors. "Man differs conspicuously from other primates in being almost naked," wrote Darwin. "But a few short straggling hairs are found over the greater part of the body in the man, and fine down on that of a woman... There can be little doubt that the hairs thus scattered over the body are the rudiments of the uniform hairy coat of the lower animals."[6]

Now, apes are vegetarian, but we became omnivore so that we could eat not only vegetables but other animals, including humans. And we did this in order to grow stronger, to survive and to mate so that we could produce more humans, thus perpetuating the species. Theory of evolution postulates that the primary goal of a species, even if the species does not have a clue about it, is to make more of it for no apparent reason or purpose.

Somewhere in the process of our ape-human metamorphosis or long after it, we developed self-awareness or self-consciousness, a unique phenomenon that allows us to know that we are a certain individual, not the other—and this is what sets us apart from lower animals. However, neither evolution theory nor any other theory can enlighten us as to how this consciousness struck the brain of the first human or how it was passed from one human to its offspring through natural selection, and then spread throughout humanity.

Which gene or set of genes by itself and within itself or a brain region developed this immaterial, invisible element that makes us know that we are human *B* rather than human *A*? Regardless how it happened, we humans developed, not only self-awareness, but, in time, an immense degree of intelligence and all sorts of talents and skills—mathematical, artistic, musical genius, humor, wit, and philosophical musings and so many others, all of which with no apparent advantage in a world where fitness was the engine of survival. Surrounded by a pack of hungry wolves, I doubt playing the violin or reciting Shakespeare to them would save your life!

When I said if a scientist put a *spirit* in a human being it may cost his tenure, I was not kidding. Wallace, a prominent naturalist and one of the leading evolutionary thinkers of the nineteenth century, could not find, in the theory he himself and Darwin discovered, how natural selection accounted for the emergence of the non-material higher mental faculties present in humans, which give us those talents and skills mentioned above. "Neither natural selection nor the more general theory of evolution can give any account whatever in the origin of sensational or conscious life,"[7] he wrote. Wallace could not conceive how chance, genetic errors or environmental adaptation could give rise to such phenomena. So how could it have happened if not by a fluke of nature as postulated by Darwinian Theory? Wallace concluded that through different degrees of spiritual influx supernatural forces had come into action at least three times in the history of life: in the initial origin of organic life; in the creation of sensation and consciousness in higher animals; and in the shaping of certain human faculties, such as morality and cultural intelligence.[8] Wallace believed that the objective of the universe was the development of the human spirit.

The second half of the nineteenth century, the years that Darwin and Wallace introduced their theory, was also the period that saw the birth of Modern Spiritualism as a new religion in America. Spiritualism spread like wildfire throughout the world, and was practiced and scientifically investigated in England by such scientists and scholars as William Crookes, Frank Podmore, Frederick Myers, William Barrett and other luminaries of the time, including Wallace.

Wallace had become a Spiritualist, something materialistic science could not swallow. Though his theory had some sympathizers, he was ostracized from the scientific establishment, and lived broke his entire life, which was quite long, ninety years. When I said if a scientist gets at all close to a term smacking of spirit it is heresy, I was not kidding either. Wallace was known as the *heretic scientist* because of the "great many eccentric and fringe causes [he] championed throughout his career."[9]

Thus Darwin's theory of soulless humans prevailed in the scientific community, since his was more rational than Wallace's superstitious confabulations. Henceforth, human beings became seen as physiological machines. There was no greater purpose in life other than to procreate and to perpetuate the species—God knows for what reason—to adapt to the environment where they happen to be born or moved to, and to struggle for survival until the day death comes and annihilates them for all eternity.

And this is how conventional science sees us to this day. There is nothing in a human being, be it Aristotle, Mozart, Shakespeare,

Einstein, Edison, Picasso, you and me, other than our physical body. The existence of a soul or spirit that can survive physical death is a fantasy we create in order to escape the fear of death we are naturally born with. Therefore, the explanation conventional science gives to NDEs and their accompanying elements such as feeling of leaving the physical body, traveling through a tunnel, meeting deceased relatives and friends, life review and so forth are productions of the brain. And the reason why the brain produces such fantasies, say brain scientists, is to make death a more palatable experience. But where exactly in the brain are these fantasies produced?

Digging the Brain

"Which part of the brain produces NDE?" scientists have asked. The right temporal lobe is the strongest candidate. However, in a great number of NDEs no lobe is working, including the right; in fact, the brain is flatlined. As we have seen previously, a brain flatlines when it produces no electric activity, and lack of electric activity in the brain means that not a sliver of brain function is possible, not even the thought of a *dot*, let alone such complex, coherent, sequentially organized, sensorially rich experiences such as we see in NDEs. Some of which, like Pam Reynolds's, for instance, had enough material to be a script for a big screen movie.

The right temporal lobe hypothesis has its origins in the work of Canadian neurosurgeon Wilder Penfield, in the 1950s to 1960s. To treat patients with epilepsy he stimulated the Sylvian fissure in the right temporal lobe. The patients, who were kept awake during the procedure, would tell Penfield what they were feeling. And some reported they felt like leaving their body.

Currently, a leading proponent of this hypothesis is Swiss neurologist Dr. Olaf Blanke. In 2002, he was treating a woman who suffered from epilepsy. The treatment involved the stimulation with electrodes of a region of the brain called the angular gyrus, which is involved in perception. At a point during the procedure the woman told Blanke she felt out of her body, and could see it down below. Blanke wrote a paper that was published in the prestigious medical journal *Nature*.[10] Later he carried on similar experiments in six patients, and published the results in 2004, in the journal *Brain*. These patients also reported sensations of "floating, flying, elevation, rotation, visual body-part illusions,"[11] wrote Blanke. One patient reported seeing a green meadow and hill, another saw the physical body in bed, still another perceived someone behind him who was not there, another saw an image of herself in front of her eyes, and these were the most dramatic events Blanke found in the experiments. Keep in mind that the patients were all awake and conscious; and they spoke to the experimenters as they electrically stimulated the patients' brains. The patients interacted with the experimenters from the physical body's perspective, as consciousness remained focused in the brain. As opposed to what happens during a NDE when consciousness moves to the spirit body.

Blanke and other neuroscientists are doing such experiments to prove that there is nothing supernatural or spiritual in NDE, OBE, or in humans. Moreover—and sadly—Blanke calls these sensations "pathological", caused by some sort of mental disorder. What Blanke and like-minded scientists do not know is that their experiments are not disproving the existence of an independent consciousness, but proving it! And we must urge them to continue! If their patients *floated* above their physical body and *saw* it down below, from the ceiling, they could have not *seen* whatever was under with their physical eyes! Unless they were being held upside down, it was just impossible. And nobody on this earth could know it better than a brain scientist! Blanke's patients could have only seen what was down below from a point above them, and with some kind of non-physical visual mechanism, independently from the physical eyes. NDErs and OBErs see their body lying below when they are out by this mechanism. But unlike the epileptic patients in these experiments, the locus of consciousness during a NDE or OBE is in the spirit body, since the physical is torpid.

The late Robert Monroe, a prolific OBEr, achieved worldwide recognition for his explorations of the OBE phenomenon. His book, *Journeys Out of the Body*, published in 1971, popularized the term "out-of-body experience". A radio broadcast executive, he began researching specific sound patterns which could facilitate OBE. With the help of specialists in psychology, medicine, biochemistry, psychiatry, electrical engineering, physics, and education, he developed a sound system he patented as Hemi-Sync, which I have used with great success. The sounds are incredibly pleasant, structured to lower brain frequency, to deeply relax the body so that we, in our spirit body, can exit it at will. Monroe's idea behind Hemi-Sync sound technology was to stimulate regions in the brain (perhaps the right temporal lobe?) that would allow the OBEr an easier exit from the physical body.

Therefore, what we can infer from Penfield's, Monroe's, and Blanke's experiments (to name a few) is not that stimulation of certain brain areas produces an illusion that a person is out of their body—on the contrary. We can infer (and scientifically test) that there are artificial means to stimulate certain areas of the brain that could facilitate our exit from the physical body, which we already do naturally, mainly when the body sleeps. The key to leaving the physical body in a more complete manner is to render it torpid, which we can accomplish by deep relaxation. Easier than that is when the entire system shuts down, such as in NDE, followed by complete emancipation when the body dies for good. So far, neuroscience, Blanke and the entire debunker community are quite far from giving the last word on the veracity of NDE, OBE, and survival of the human spirit, soul, or consciousness.

Wilder Penfield, whose temporal lobe stimulation in epileptic patients inspired Blanke and others to dismiss NDE and OBE as abnormal mental behaviors, dug deeper into the lobes than just electrode stimulation—literally! To control intractable cases of epilepsy, Penfield and Jasper, another surgeon, "routinely removed sizeable sectors of cortex in conscious patients..." [and] they were impressed by the fact that the removal of sizeable sectors of cortex... never interrupted the patient's continuity of consciousness even while the tissue was being surgically removed."[12] Even when they removed the entire hemisphere (half brain) consciousness continued. As you recall, neuroscientists believe that the cortex produces consciousness; therefore, if pieces of cortex are removed, let alone half of the brain, consciousness should also discontinue. But it did not.

In a brief period of two years, Blanke stimulated the brain of seven epileptic patients (one in 2002 and six until 2004). These patients reported fleeting feelings of leaving the body, floating upwards, flying, seeing the physical body. And this was enough evidence to convince Blanke that there is no such thing as consciousness being independent of the physical brain, such as NDE and OBE imply.

Penfield, on the other hand, spent over thirty years searching for the brain area which produced consciousness or mind. His treatments and experiments on epileptics numbered 750! In his book The Mystery of the Mind, published in 1975, shortly before his death, he concluded:

To suppose that consciousness or the mind has localization is a failure to understand neurophysiology...[13] For myself, after a professional lifetime spent trying to discover how the brain accounts for the mind, it comes as a surprise now to discover, during this final examination of the evidence, that the dualist hypothesis (separation of mind and brain) seems the more reasonable of the two possible explanations...[14]Mind comes into action and goes out of action with the highest brain-mechanism, it is true. But the mind has energy. The form of that energy is different from that of neuronal potentials that travel the axon pathways. There I must leave it.[15]

Penfield's extensive experiments and conclusions, and NDE and OBE phenomena, make it very clear that neuroscience, Blanke included, is quite far from giving the last word—that we are just perishable physical bodies with not much reason for existing. If you believe that you are an immortal being but see your faith shaking when reading about a scientific experiment giving a reductionist explanation, such as Blanke's, or any other materialistic scientist, affirming they have just discovered there is nothing immortal in our human nature, keep your faith. Though science is incredibly advanced in many areas, in others, such as in consciousness research, it's just speculating, and such speculations may be way off mark, as abundantly verified in the very history of science.

Our Double Nature

Alfred Russell Wallace, the co-discoverer of evolutionary processes of animals and humans, contrary to Charles Darwin, did not believe we are purposeless and perishable physiological machines. To him:

1. Man is a duality, consisting of an organized spiritual form, evolved coincidently and permeating the physical body, and having corresponding organs and development.
2. Death is the separation of this duality, and effects no change in the spirit, morally or intellectually.
3. Progressive evolution of the intellectual and moral nature is the destiny of individuals; the knowledge, attainments, and experience of earth-life forming the basis of spirit-life.[16]

Echoing Wallace, *Spiritism* holds that when we are experiencing life on earth we are:

...composed of body and Spirit; the Spirit is the primary, the rational and the intelligent being (the part of us which leaves the body during NDE and OBE!); the body is the material encasement which hosts, temporarily, the Spirit (us!) so that we can carry on our earthly mission and perform our evolutionary work. The physical and spiritual states are, to the Spirit, two sources of progress which work together simultaneously; thus the reason why we alternate these two modes of existence.[17]

Earth is a great school to us as spirit, and the body is the physical uniform we must don while here. Life on earth offers wonderful learning opportunities for our moral, spiritual and intellectual development. In the words of Emmanuel, "Earth must be considered a fraternal school for the advancement and regeneration of incarnate Spirits."[18]

Before this incarnation we lived, in our spirit body, in the non-physical or spiritual realm, which is all around us, occupying the same space where we live our physical life. To experience life on earth we needed a denser body that allowed us to interact with other incarnate spirits and objects peculiar to material life. Though we, as spirit, are tightly connected to the physical body during our incarnation, we can function independently and do leave it sometimes. NDEs and OBEs are eloquent testimonials of this independence. Though we seem to be composed of only one element—the physical body—we have, while incarnated on earth, a double nature, physical and spiritual. Upon the death of the physical body, we return to our original state—that of free spirit—until that blessed time we come back again for another round. And so goes the dance of life in an eternal continuum, always moving forward, forever giving us opportunities to learn and grow.

Conclusion

In the current stage of our consciousness evolution, we sometimes need to experience pain to shake us out of the torpor material life imposes on us as spirit. Though we are spirit and not a physical body, our limited senses, beliefs, prejudices, vanity, and most commonly our ignorance, prevent us from reviewing our life on a daily basis while we are still on the earthly plane; and redirecting it when and where needed without having to undergo such a drastic wake-up call as a NDE. As we have seen in the few cases in this book—and there are more cases than we have time to read or to listen to in this lifetime—people who reviewed their lives during a NDE saw their mistakes and recognized the need to change their conduct. However, as it was not their time to (physically) die, they returned and many made the necessary changes to correct their mistakes, living a more fulfilling life than prior to having a NDE. They found pleasure in helping others; lived a more spiritual life; became more loving and forgiving toward others. They also pursued knowledge; focused on doing good deeds; and learned to accept others and themselves as they were.

And how about those people whose time has come? Over 150,000 souls around the world cross over to the other side of life every day! They will certainly review their lives at some point, see the mistakes they have made, the suffering they might have caused, which they may bitterly regret and want to return to earth to redeem their faults. But they cannot. Their physical bodies are dead and they cannot return to them. How would that make them feel, in the depths of their soul, in the core of their consciousness, before such impossibility?

Now, what if one of *those people* were you or me? Our time will come, we can be certain of that, and it could be today, in a few hours, or a few minutes. We all know that no living being will escape physical death. We are at the mercy of it at every moment. Our return ticket has been issued from that sublime moment we took the first breath in this bittersweet earthly experience. We are just waiting boarding time, which can happen without prior notice. Death does not care if our luggage is ready or not, and can and often does, using the popular adage, catch us with our pants down—literally in many cases.

There is only one way to avoid being caught with our pants down when our time comes. How? Living our life like God told Lynn during her NDE, "Live in such a way that you will not feel bad when you return here again." And this is done by loving others as we love ourselves, as Jesus taught us; learning and practicing forgiveness; doing good as much as we can; being compassionate towards and understanding of others' weaknesses and limitations; being peaceful and fostering peace; living moral lives; and acquiring knowledge are just a few examples—for the good of no other than our own selves!

The life review phase we have seen in the various accounts presented gives us an idea of how our own encounter with our spirit guides might be when our time comes. We have seen that the Being of Light or God or Jesus or whoever it may be is quite understanding and neither judges nor condemns our wrong-doings. But our consciousness does! It must be painful and shameful for us being in the presence of such enlightened figures watching in 3D our sordid actions, our rudeness, our vices, and offenses we perpetrated towards our loved ones and friends who loved us, the evil we have done when we should not have, and the good we failed to do when we should have. Obviously, not all of our actions are vile; we have certainly performed noble and dignifying deeds as well. But about these we must not brag. Doing good and living right is our obligation. It is a commitment we have with our Creator. And besides, we are the ones to be benefited the most by our own righteous living. Cause and effect is an inexorable law no one can escape from. Any action we take will generate a reaction which can give us pleasure or pain depending on its nature. We might or might not feel the impact right away, but it will catch up with us either in this life or in the next. The Apostle Paul had it very clear when he wrote to the Galatians, "Be not deceived; God is not mocked: for whatsoever man sows, that shall he also reap."[1]

A great number of NDErs report that they discovered the hard way what Paul meant by these words, feeling in the core of their being the veracity of this statement. But as it was not their time to stay on the other side of life, they returned to earth and changed their old ways. They learned the real reason why we have come to this earth—to learn to love, to forgive, to do good, to revere life, not only human life but all life in all forms. They discovered the huge family humanity is, and many felt in their own soul the pain they caused their fellow humans and other sentient beings they might have hurt.

It is my hope that the experiences NDErs brought to us from the other side of life serve us well. May they be warnings, inspiring us to a serious examination of our current moral and ethical conduct; prompting us to take a moment every day to assess the quality of our actions, of our attitudes, and our feelings not only towards our loved ones and close friends, but also towards all humanity. May these experiences speak loudly to our hearts and set us on the path that leads to God. And when our turn comes to cross the barrier of no return, in that sublime moment the Being of Light, whoever it is, appears before us, he will not even have to ask, "What have you done with your life to show me?" He will see our greatness radiating on the brilliant light emanating from our being.

References

Chapter 1: We Are More Than Human

1. Pierre Teilhard de Chardin, *The Phenomenon of Man* (New York: Harper Perennial, 1965), 63.

2. Harold Saxton Burr, *Blueprint of Immortality: The Electric Patterns of Life* (Essex, England: CW Daniel Co., 1991), 114.

3. Hans Driesch, *The History and Theory of Vitalism* (Forgotten Books, 2012), 31, 107.

4. Burr, *Blueprint of Immortality*, 11.

5. Burr, *Blueprint of Immortality*, 13.

6. Rupert Sheldrake, *Morphic Resonance: The Nature of Formative Causation* (Rochester, VT: Park Street Press, 2009), 3.

7. Chardin, *The Phenomenon of Man*, 62.

Chapter 2: The Perks of Being Free

1. 1 Corinthians 15:51–55 (King James Version).

2. 1 Corinthians 15:44 (KJV).

Chapter 3: The Science of OBE

1. Patent number 836524. Filing date: Jun 14, 1904. Issue date: Nov 20, 1906.
http://www.google.com/patents/US836524

2. Ed Morrell, *The 25th Man: The Strange Story of Ed. Morrell, the Hero of Jack London's Star Rover* (Montclair, NJ: New Era, 1924), 325–326.

3. Morrell, *The 25th Man*, 369.

4. Michael Talbot, *The Holographic Universe* (New York: HarperPerennial, 1991), 240.

5. Charles T. Tart, 1968. "A psychophysiological study of out-of-body experiences in a selected subject." *Journal of the American Society for Psychical Research*, 62:3–27.

6. David Fontana, *Is There an Afterlife? A Comprehensive*

Overview of the Evidence (Hants, England: O-Books, 2005), 413.

7. D. Scott Rogo. *Life After Death – The Case for Survival of Bodily Death* (Northamptonshire, England: The Aquarian Press, 1986), 49.

8. D. Scott Rogo, *Leaving the Body: A Complete Guide to Astral Projection* (New York: Fireside, 1983), x.

9. Rogo, Life After Death, 56-57. (Scott Rogo participated in these experiments as an advisor)

10. Rogo, *Life After Death*, 58.

11. Rogo, *Life After Death*, 58.

12. Rogo, *Life After Death*, 50.

13. Jim Schnabel, *Remote Viewers: The Secret History of America's Psychic Spies* (New York: Dell, 1997).

Chapter 4: What is Near-Death Experience (NDE) — Really?

1. Cindy L. Stanfield and William J. Germann, *Principles of Human Physiology, 3rd Edition* (San Francisco: Pearson, 2008), 360.

2. Catherine E. Myers, "Memory Loss and the Brain." *The Newsletter of the Memory Disorders Project, at Rutgers University*:
http://www.memorylossonline.com/glossary/hypoxiaanoxia.html

3. "Cardiopulmonary resuscitation":
http://en.wikipedia.org/ and
http://en.wikipedia.org/wiki/Cardiopulmonary_resuscitation

Chapter 5: NDE Everywhere

1. Raymond Moody and Paul Perry, *Glimpses of Eternity* (New York: Guideposts, 2010), 70.

2. George Gallup, Jr. and William Proctor, *Adventures in Immortality* (New York: McGraw-Hill, 1982), 6.

3. Brendan I. Koerner and Joshua Rich, "Is There Life After Death?" *US News*:
    http://www.usnews.com/usnews/culture/articles/970331/archive_006588.htm
4. Jeffrey Long, "How Many NDEs Occur in the US Every Day?": http://www.nderf.org/number_nde_usa.htm
5. PMH Atwater, *Beyond the Light: Near-Death Experiences — The Full Story* (London, UK: Thorsons, 1995), 15.
6. 1 Samuel 28:3–18 (King James Version).
7. Ibid, 28:7 (KJV).
8. Ibid, 28:19 (KJV).
9. Ibid, 31:2 (KJV).
10. Francisco C. Xavier, *O Consolador*, 18th Edition (Brasilia, Brazil: FEB, 1997), 72.

Chapter 6: Witnessing Immortality

1. Raymond Moody, Jr., *Life After Life* (Covington, GA: Mockingbird, 1975), 35.

Chapter 7: The Ten Phases of NDE

1. Margot Grey, *Return From Death: An Exploration of the Near-Death Experience* (New York: Routledge & Kegan Paul, 1986), 38.
2. Grey, *Return From Death*, 50.
3. Raymond Moody, Jr., *Life After Life* (Covington, GA: Mockingbird, 1975), 73–74.
4. Margot Grey, *Return From Death: An Exploration of the Near-Death Experience* (New York: Routledge & Kegan Paul, 1986), 82.
5. Michael Sabom, *Light & Death* (Grand Rapids, MI: Zondervan, 1998), 46.
6. Francisco C. Xavier, *O Consolador*, 18th Edition (Brasilia, Brazil: FEB, 1997), 122.
7. Sam Parnia, *What Happens When We Die: A Groundbreaking*

Study into the Nature of Life and Death (Carlsbad, CA: Hay House, 2006), 177.

Chapter 8: Brain Not Required

1. Bjorn Merker, "Consciousness without a Cerebral Cortex: A Challenge for Neuroscience and Medicine." *Behavioral and Brain Science*, 30 (2006): 63–81.

2. Cindy L. Stanfield and William J Germann, *Principles of Human Physiology, 3rd Edition* (San Francisco: Pearson, 2008), 230–231. Arthur S. Bard & Mitchell G. Bard, *Understanding the Brain* (Indianapolis: Alpha, 2002), 61.

3. Centers for Disease Control and Prevention, "Facts About Anencephaly": http://www.cdc.gov/ncbddd/birthdefects/anencephaly.html.

4. National Institute of Neurological Disorders and Strokes, Hydranencephaly Information Page: http://www.ninds.nih.gov/disorders/hydranencephaly/hydranencephaly.htm

5. Bjorn Merker, "Consciousness without a Cerebral Cortex: A Challenge for Neuroscience and Medicine." *Behavioral and Brain Science*, 30 (2006): 63–81.

6. Tatiana Pronin, "Médicos ainda não estão preparados para fazer diagnósticos como o de Vitória diz especialista." *UOL Noticias Ciência* (2012). (Translated into English by the author.): *http://noticias.uol.com.br/ciencia/ultimas-noticias/redacao/2012/04/13/* medicos-ainda-nao-estao-preparados-para-fazer-diagnosticos -como-o-de-vitoria-diz-especialista.htm

7. D. Alan Shewmon, Gregory L. Holmes, Paul A. Byrne, "Consciousness in Congenitally Decorticate Children: Developmental vegetative state as a self-fulfilling prophecy." *Developmental Medicine and Child Neurology*, 41 (1999): 364–374.

8. Ibid.

9. Arthur S. Bard & Mitchell G. Bard, *Understanding the Brain* (Indianapolis: Alpha, 2002), 64.

10. Neil R. Carlson, *Psychology: The Science of Behavior* (New Jersey, USA: Pearson Education, 2007), 115.

11. D. Alan Shewmon, Gregory L. Holmes, Paul A. Byrne, "Consciousness in Congenitally Decorticate Children: Developmental vegetative state as a self-fulfilling prophecy." *Developmental Medicine and Child Neurology*, 41 (1999): 364–374.

12. National Institute of Neurological Disorders and Strokes, Hydranencephaly Information Page: http://www.ninds.nih.gov/disorders/hydranencephaly/hydranencephaly.htm

13. Arthur S. Bard & Mitchell G. Bard, *Understanding the Brain* (Indianapolis: Alpha, 2002), 3.

14. "Miracle child born without brain dies in Pueblo": http://www.koaa.com/news/miracle-child-born-without-brain-dies-in-pueblo/

15. "Beloved Victoria Blogspot", http://belovedvitoria.blogspot.com/

16. Ibid.

Chapter 9: More Than Meets the Eye

1. Michael Sabom, *Light & Death* (Grand Rapids, MI: Zondervan, 1998), 37.

2. Sabom, *Light & Death*, 37–46.

3. Allan Kardec, *The Spirits' Book* (Rio de Janeiro, Brazil: FEB, 1996), 208.

4. Kimberly Clark Sharp, *After the Light* (New York: William Morrow, 1995), 7.

5. Pim van Lommel et al. "Near-death experience in survivors of cardiac arrest: a prospective study in the Netherlands." *Lancet*, 358 (2001), 2039–45.

6. David Fontana, *Is There an Afterlife?* (Hants, UK: O-Books, 2005), 395.

7. Maurice Rawlings, *Beyond Death's Door* (New York: Bantam, 1975), 29.

Chapter 10: Through the Soul's Eyes — NDE of the Blind

1. Kenneth Ring and Sharon Cooper, *Mindsight: Near-Death and Out-of-Body Experiences in the Blind* (Palo Alto, CA: William James Center for Consciousness Studies, Institute of Transpersonal Psychology, 1999), 22.

2. Ring and Cooper, *Mindsight*, 30.

3. John 9:2–3 (King James Version).

4. Ring and Cooper, *Mindsight*, 81.

5. Ring and Cooper, *Mindsight*, 74.

6. Rustum Roy in *The New Science and Spirituality Reader*, edited by Ervin Laszlo and Kingsley L. Dennis (Rochester, VT: Inner Traditions, 2012), 17.

7. Matthew 5:48 (King James Version).

Chapter 11: A Bitter Taste of Nothingness

1. Barbara R. Rommer, *Blessing in Disguise* (St. Paul, MN: Llewellyn, 2000), 42.

2. Maurice Rawlings, *Beyond Death's Door* (New York: Bantam, 1975), 90.

3. Galatians 6:7 (King James Version).

4. *Blessing in Disguise*, 48.

5. Matthew 7:7–8 (KJV).

6. From Elton John's song *Circle of Life*.

Chapter 12: Suicide, a Mistaken Choice

1. Centers for Disease Control and Prevention, "Suicide, Facts at a Glance":
http://www.cdc.gov/violenceprevention/pdf/Suicide-Data Sheet-a.pdf

2. Bruce Greyson and Nancy E. Bush, "Distressing Near-Death Experiences." *Psychiatry*, 55 (1992): 105.

3. Barbara R. Rommer, *Blessing in Disguise* (St. Paul, MN: Llewellyn, 2000), 47.

4. Rommer, *Blessing in Disguise*, 56.

5. Francisco C. Xavier, *O Consolador, 18th Edition* (Brasilia, Brazil: FEB, 1997), 96.

Chapter 13: Overdose, a Hellish Trip

1. Barbara R. Rommer, *Blessing in Disguise* (St. Paul, MN: Llewellyn, 2000), 78.

2. Rommer, *Blessing in Disguise*, 91.

3. Ephesians 4:22–24 (King James Version).

4. Matthew 7:12 (King James Version).

Chapter 14: Children Near Death

1. Melvin Morse and Paul Perry, *Closer to the Light: Learning from the Near-Death Experiences of Children* (New York: Ivy Books, 1991), 3.

2. Morse and Perry, Closer to the Light, 5.

3. Ibid.

4. Morse and Perry, *Closer to the Light*.

5. Sam Parnia, *What Happens When We Die: A Groundbreaking Study into the Nature of Life and Death* (Carlsbad, CA: Hay House, 2006), 75.

6. *When Angels Intervene to Save the Children* by Hartt and Judene Wixom is an extraordinary example.

7. PMH Atwater, *Children of the New Millennium* (New York: Three Rivers, 1999), 15.

8. Atwater, *Children of the New Millennium*, 39.

9. Melvin Morse and Paul Perry, *Where God Lives* (New York: HarperCollins, 2000), 3.

10. Atwater, *Children of the New Millennium*, 61.

Chapter 15: Cheating the Grim Reaper?

1. Maggie Callanan and Patricia Kelley, *Final Gifts: Understanding the Special Awareness, Needs, and Communications of the Dying* (New York: Bantam, 1992), 197.
2. Bruce Greyson and Nancy E. Bush, "Distressing Near-Death Experiences." *Psychiatry*, 55 (1992): 99.
3. Francisco C. Xavier, *O Consolador*, 18th Edition (Brasilia, Brazil: FEB, 1997), 72.
4. Raymond Moody and Paul Perry, *Glimpses of Eternity* (New York: Guideposts, 2010), 8.

Chapter 16: Our Double Nature

1. Brian Swimme and Thomas Berry, *The Universe Story: From the Primordial Flaring Forth to the Ecozoic Era* (San Francisco: HarperCollins, 1992), 8.
2. Luigi Luca Cavalli-Sforza and Francesco Cavalli-Sforza, *The Great Human Diasporas: The History of Diversity and Evolution* (New York: Addison-Wesley Publishing, 1995), 79.
3. Barbara Marx Hubbard in *The New Science and Spirituality Reader*, edited by Ervin Laszlo and Kingsley L. Dennis (Rochester, VT: Inner Traditions, 2012), 57.
4. Charles Darwin, *The Origin of Species* (New York: Signet Classics, 2003), 4.
5. Brian Swimme and Thomas Berry, *The Universe Story* (New York: HarperSan Francisco, 1994), 148.
6. Charles Darwin, *The Descent of Man* (Seattle: Madison Park, 2011), 14.
7. Michael Shermer, *In Darwin's Shadow: The Life and Science of Alfred Russell Wallace* (New York: Oxford University Press, 2002), 230.
8. Shermer, *In Darwin's Shadow*, 230.
9. Shermer, *In Darwin's Shadow*, xvii.
10. Olaf Blanke et al., "Neuropsychology: Stimulating Illusory Own-Body Perceptions." *Nature*, 419 (2002): 269–270.

11. Olaf Blanke et al., "Out-of-Body Experience and Autoscopy of Neurological Origin." *Brain*, 127 (2004).

12. Bjorn Merker, "Consciousness Without a Cerebral Cortex: A Challenge for Neuroscience and Medicine," Behavioral and Brain Science 30 (2006): 63-81.

13. Wilder Penfield, *The Mystery of The Mind* (Princeton, NJ: Princeton University Press, 1975), 109.

14. Penfield, *The Mystery of the Mind*, 114.

15 Penfield, *The Mystery of the Mind*, 48.

16. Shermer, *In Darwin's Shadow*, 23.

17. Allan Kardec, *O Céu e o Inferno* (Araras, São Paulo, Brazil: Instituto de Difusão Espírita, 2003), 28

18. Francisco C. Xavier, *O Consolador, 18th Edition* (Brasilia, Brazil: FEB, 1997), 197.

Conclusion

1. Galatians 6:7 (King James Version).

BOOKS

6th Books investigates the paranormal, supernatural, explainable or unexplainable. Titles cover everything included within parapsychology: how to, lifestyles, beliefs, myths, theories and memoir.